Books by Bill Thesken

The Lords of Xibalba
The Oil Eater
Blocking Paris
Window

Edge of the Pit

Bill Thesken

First Edition Published 2016
Koloa Publishing, LLC
www.koloapublishing.com
P.O. Box 1609
Koloa, HI 96756

Book cover designed by Deranged Doctor Design

ISBN 978-0-9903519-5-5
ISBN 0-9903519-5-5

1.

My name is Badger Thompson.

I work for a protection service. Our clients are the richest people in the country, the top one percenters, and they pay a lot of money to stay safe.

It's getting near midnight and I've been on location since it got dark a few hours ago, huddled in the middle of a large bush near enough to the mansion to see all the entrances and most of the property surrounding it. I use the infrared scope to scan the property and then listen. Scan and listen.

I carry three identical handguns, loaded with the safeties off, extra ammo on my belt, two boot knives, a couple of stun grenades, a hand held Taser, and a few canisters of the all-around useful pepper spray.

My old man had a saying when I was growing up, used to tell it to me all the time: "Nothing good happens after midnight son, that's when the shit hits the fan."

Trying to scare me, or warn me to stay out of

trouble, stay away from the bottom half of the night. I didn't listen very well.

The old man had a lot of sayings, and he wasn't right about everything, but he sure as hell was right about that one.

I do a lot of my work at night, some of it after midnight and I've seen the fan in action a few times. You never really know when someone's gonna hit the 'on' switch and you gotta be ready at all times.

I'm the guy on the edge of the crowd, the guy you never see, never notice, never even hear about. I watch the perimeter and look out for the bad guys.

They put me on the edge of houses, parties, events. I'm like an early warning device for a tsunami or a nuclear attack, only I don't just warn.

They put me on the edge for a reason. I can blend in, make myself invisible and take out trouble like most people take out the trash. I know how the bad guys think, how they look, how they move, what they're capable of. I know because once upon a time I was the bad guy, and could still be one at the drop of a hat, or a bullet.

The bad guys work at night, so we work at night. Like a cat against a rat. They rotate us in and out like pieces of a machine, watching, ever watching, on the perimeter. Always on the perimeter. Sometimes we have to spring into action, but it's rare, and we can't watch everyone all the time, we burn out like anything else, get tired, need sleep.

I'm the guy on the edge, in more ways than one. There's a few good ones, and I'm one of the best there is. For now that is. You can never be the best forever, but for now I'm about as close as anyone will get.

The bodyguards, the close circle of protection next to the client, they know I'm out here, somewhere, they just don't know where I'm at, or what I look like, who I am. I come and go like a shadow, or a wisp of the wind. Like a myth that's talked about quietly in the dark of night for fear of someone hearing.

It's better that way, gives an extra layer of protection for the client. The less people know about the guys on the perimeter, the better it is for everyone. We don't get in their way, and they don't get in ours. We're an unknown quantity as far as the bad guys are concerned. If they knew about us, they'd prepare for us, and we can't have that. The perimeter is like the wild zone, a no man's land, we're on our own out here, and we don't want anyone to point us out and say, 'See look over there, our force protection is out in front, we're safe here in this circle.' We'd be sitting ducks out here.

It's gotta be like this: we're the ones coming in silent and secret and unknown and hitting the bad guys before they can hit us, before they even know what the hell happened to them.

When I was seventeen my Dad passed away. Hit me like a brick to the head. It happened so suddenly that I never had time to say goodbye.

It's a tough time for any kid in the dangerous late teen years when you need someone to talk to, look up to, and I took it pretty hard. All stability in my life was gone.

My Grandpa moved in and tried to fill the gap, but it wasn't the same. He was old and grumpy and set in his ways and we had a hard time talking. I started running with a gang in the ugly part of town, drinking and fighting and battling the other gangs, thought I was a tough guy. I was young and angry and stupid.

My Grandpa found out I was skipping school and dragged me by the scruff of my neck down to the Army recruitment center and signed me up. One year later I was in Baghdad during the surge, living in the Green Zone during the day in an air-conditioned bomb proof shelter, and at night going out to the city with my platoon, busting down doors and rounding up the bad guys.

Half the people in the city hated us, and wanted to kill us. The other half also hated us, but just wanted to be left alone. It was hard to tell by looking at them which was which since they all looked the same. Except when they were shooting at us or throwing grenades in our general direction, then you could tell who the trouble makers were, and that's why we were there, to calm things down and restore some semblance of law and order that we obliterated in the invasion. To fix a broken machine if that was even possible. Put it all back together again so we could get the hell out of there.

We didn't look the same or speak their language or understand their customs, and make a mistake, make one false move and you're dead. But, we had the best weapons and night vision gear that money could buy, and a city full of bad characters. It was more excitement than any guy my age should be allowed.

Usually the Intel we got was pretty good and we kept our casualties to a minimum. But every once in a while we got juiced and had to fight our way in or out, and we had to keep a tight group. There were enemy snipers and car bombs, improvised explosive devices buried next to every road in the country, ambushes, mortar attacks, rocket propelled grenades, and a lot of angry people surrounding you on every street corner, you could see it their eyes, they were occupied and given the chance would cut your head off. Being in a little gang back home was kids' stuff compared to Baghdad.

Johnny was sick one night with a high fever and pneumonia, and they put me on the perimeter. I spotted something suspicious and disarmed a sniper before he knew what hit him, and I stayed on the perimeter for the rest of my tour. I was really good at it, and when I got out of the Army, the agency looked me up and signed me to a team.

The money is good, and I'm working hard and saving every penny so I can buy two small yachts, a sailboat and a power boat so I can start my own business providing boat rides and security in one bundle. I'll call the sailboat

'Sugar', and the power boat 'Spice', and I'll provide the service for the top ten percenters. The one percenters are turning out to be a pain in the rear, and probably wouldn't be caught dead on a piddly quarter million dollar scow anyways.

They pay me a grand per day and let me work up to five per week so I'm crisp and alert, and ready for action. That's a cool quarter million per year, and I'm getting close to my goal of half a million for the boats. It's taken almost four years, what with all the tax collectors riding my back like a monkey after a banana.

The crickets are loud tonight. It's pitch black dark with no moon, the stars hidden by an overcast sky of high clouds and no wind. Sound travels far in these conditions and I use it to my advantage. The crickets are my friends, like sentinels in the night, and when they stop singing I know something is moving near them, or they're cautious. It could be nothing, and it could be everything. The Indians used the birds of the forest for hunting, they could understand the language in a way that's long been lost, know when certain animals, or their enemies were nearby. Nights like this I use the crickets, and the wind. Like a blind man feels the change of volume in a room from confined to cavernous I hear the subtle change of sounds. It's an acquired skill. From working at night.

It's a huge sprawling property on the edge of suburban sprawl which is itself on the edge of the giant city. Fenced and gated, five square acres, an oasis of trees and lawns and open space, long winding brick driveways bordered with flowers.

Bentleys and Mercedes are parked in front of the house which looks like it could host one hell of a party. Modern Victorian with long tall windows, gabled roofs and covered patios at each side.

She opened the door and stood in the light, holding it open for a moment like she was standing on a stage. The star. Her hair was long and golden brown, flowing over the white evening gown and down her shoulders, pouting lips, soft cheeks. This girl has it all, tawny skin, sultry look, and the kind of attitude that says I have it going on and I know that you know it.

Feelings like molasses, sweet and honey thick choked my gut, and I got rid of them quickly.

She's the rich guy's friend, so they sent us to escort her to the destination safely. It's a job. Get the package from one point to another, and then back again. Like the US Postal service. Easy.

She sweeps down the staircase holding the hem of her long white dress with one hand and her purse with other and walked towards one of the shiny black Bentley's, the bigger of the two in front. The chauffeur bowed and held the door open for her, he actually bowed. If I didn't see it with the scope I wouldn't have believed it. Like he was bowing to the Queen of England. One of the bodyguards, a burly character built like a keg of beer in a suit and tie, climbed into the front passenger seat of the bigger Bentley, while the other two got into a another smaller Bentley behind it and I can barely hear the engines come to life. Smooth as silk.

They're on the move. I scan the perimeter again with the infrared scope, looking for trouble and seeing nothing. I'm the forward advance guy, and I'm on the move way in front of them, jogging silently through the trees to my transportation for the evening.

They're heading to a party, a late one at some rap club downtown in the gritty belly of the city. Why in the hell someone would want to go to a party after midnight in a sleazy club downtown was beyond me. They probably never heard my Dad's old saying.

I slide through the tree line and hop on the chopper that's sitting on the street below, and as I rev the motor, the un-muffled blast of pure gas combustion engine, a double banger, the two pistons firing obnoxious and loud as I can make it, the people standing across the street look at me with a mixture of reactions ranging from fear and admiration to disgust. Mostly it's fear though. A strange biker with bulging muscles and a torn leather jacket revving a Harley near midnight outside your driveway will do that to people. It's a Friday night and I nod towards them and roar off in a blast of exhaust and head to the thoroughfare. The long driveway that winds down from the mansion connects to the highway and I pull in behind the two Bentley's as they race down the road ahead of me.

They're moving at a good clip, around sixty five, well over the speed limit. A little twist of the accelerator grip and I blow by them and put some distance between us, but I keep one eye on them in the rear view mirror. It's clear up ahead and we're coming up to an intersection. I pass through it just as it's turning yellow. Bad timing. They're too far back and have to stop at the light, and I slow down a bit to keep them in sight. I'm coming to a curve in the road and gear down quickly so my brake light won't alert anyone that I'm slowing down.

I can see two large SUV's hemming the Bentley in on each side, and when another large SUV pulls right in front of them and stops I realize they're in trouble. It's a classic box maneuver. I swing the chopper around and gun it full throttle for the intersection. I can see muzzles pointed at the windshield, stun grenades and flashes. I'm still a few hundred yards away and closing, and a flash of light blinds me and I feel like I'm floating through the air, just floating and floating, effortless and free, not a care in the world, except there's an elephant sitting on my chest, and my head is in a vice grip, and there's an annoying beeping sound.....

2.

"He's waking up."

The elephant is not only sitting on my chest, he's sitting on my eyelids and I struggle to open them. It's blinding white. I'm in a room. Turns out the damn elephant isn't only sitting on my eyelids he's also sitting on my brain and I'm struggling to understand what I'm looking at. The elephant has a face and he's looking down at me, two, three of them are looking down at me, no wonder it's so damned heavy, there's three of 'em. There's tubes hanging from bottles and stretched towards my body. I try to raise my head. Why the hell does that light have to be so damned bright? And where's my motorcycle? The annoying beeping sound is coming from my right side and I see the big box with the flickering green lights, and numbers, wires coming down towards me, attached to me.

Uh oh. I'm in a hospital. I remember what this is like. The weirdest feeling in the whole damn world. I'm waking up, someone just said that and it wasn't me. It came from one of the elephants standing on me and looking down at me. I try to raise my head again and say something but my brain still won't start up, it won't connect to my lips. I can't feel my lips moving. What the hell is going on here?

"Take it easy buddy, easy now. Increase the dose nurse. He's coming out of it."

I blink again and focus on the guy doing the talking, in the white coat, a clean shaven Asian guy, he's got a stethoscope hanging from his neck and thick eyeglasses and a loud voice.

My brain is starting up, and I manage a small sound like a whistle that starts and stops and I don't know where the sound is coming from or how to control it.

"What...?" It feels like my whole body is in an echo chamber and my tongue is coated with sand. "What..." I try again.

"Take it easy okay? You've been in an accident but you're alright now. You're safe here in our hospital. You're going to be okay."

He brought his hand by my nose and pointed a bright flashlight into my eyes. I tried to close them but he was holding them open with his fat fingers and shining the light into the back of my skull.

What the hell is wrong with this guy... I blinked a few more times in rapid action and the room came into view. I was sitting halfway propped up on a bed, there were tubes and wires connected all over me. There were two white coated guys looking down at me and one super-hot nurse, I couldn't help but look at her, and that brought my brain quickly into focus, she increased the dosage, someone had said that out loud. She sure as hell did increase the dosage.

"That's enough nurse," said the Asian guy, and she stepped away from the bed. This Asian guy was beginning to get on my nerves.

"You've been in an accident son, and we had to put you in a coma for a couple of days to let the swelling go down. You've got three broken ribs, multiple contusions, and a concussion..."

My senses are coming back to me. A couple of days he said. What does that mean, two, three days, a week?

Some peoples idea of a couple of days can vary. I open my mouth and try to turn my head to the side. My head is wedged between two thick pieces of foam, the vice grip. The nurse leans over me and takes the foam away, she's full figured and even though the name on her tag says Amber, she smells like strawberries and I rotate my neck and look around. I'm in a basic one person hospital room, maybe a little bigger than a closet, and square, there's a tiny bathroom in the corner, a television hanging from the ceiling, and two guys dressed in black suits and ties leaning against a wall, watching me. A burly guy with a face like a ham sandwich and a short skinny guy wearing reflective sunglasses. Now who in the hell wears sunglasses inside? Some damn asshole who doesn't want you to see his eyes.

"How are you feeling?" asked the Asian doc.

I opened my mouth again and thought I'd give it another try. "Like... I got... run over... by a truck."

He smiled at that, must have gotten a kick out of it in fact. "Well at least you can talk. Can you say the first ten letters of the alphabet?"

"This... a... test?" I managed. "Alright," I swallowed, "the first ten letters... of the alphabet." Telling him exactly what he asked me to say.

He smiled wryly at that, and then patted me on the shoulder and motioned to the two suits. "He's all yours. We'll be back to tuck him in when you're done." He turned to me again. "You'll be with us for a couple of days, we want to monitor your condition. These gentlemen need to ask you some questions. Just don't get too agitated, okay? We'll be back when they're done to give you something to sleep again."

The two doctors and the nurse left the room and one of the suits locked the door, and they both pulled up chairs and sat close to me. The guy with the sunglasses on took them off slowly, folded them neatly and put them in the top front pocket of his suit. I could see why he wore sunglasses inside, his eyes were tiny and gray like a weasels. I'd want to hide them too. Then the burly guy started asking me questions. Small ones at first. What did I remember, what did I see, why did I go through the yellow light. Then he got closer and asked slowly,

"Why are you still alive when the others are all dead?"

I had a question for him. "Who the hell... are you guys?"

"We're from the agency," said the one who did all the talking. The other guy just stared at me.

"What agency?"

"Funny," said the talker. "We're on your side Badger. We work for the same people as you do."

Called me by my name, but I'd never seen him before. The other guy though, looked familiar somehow, someway, but in my drugged up condition I couldn't remember when or where I'd seen him. "Does he talk?" I asked and pointed to the silent one.

"Save your strength, you've been through quite an ordeal. We just need to ask you a few more questions, and then you can go back to sleep."

I figured I was in no condition to start a fight. Hell, I could barely lift my head off the pillow and I had a splitting headache. I could use a friend or two, and maybe these guys were really here to help.

Waking up in a hospital and not remembering how you got there while getting the third degree though was making me suspicious. Who were they, and what did they want?

"The last thing I remember, I was riding

the bike, there was some kind of trouble back at the light."

"Go on."

"What happened to the others?" I asked. "What happened to the girl?"

"What makes you think something happened to the girl?"

I closed my eyes for a moment to clear the cobwebs. "Didn't you just ask me why I was still alive, when all the others were dead?"

"The bodyguards and the chauffeur are dead. That is without a single doubt true. The girl however is missing." He hesitated. "We were hoping you could tell us where she is."

I closed my eyes tight. Uh oh. Maybe I was dreaming. This was all just a dream and I was still in a coma, and this was all just a dream...just a dream... I opened my eyes and they were still there, watching me. Not a dream.

"I'm the guy who just woke up from a coma, and you're asking *me* if I know where she is?"

The talker didn't say anything, just nodded slowly while the silent one stared with gray eyes.

"So you're telling me that the guys are all dead, and the girl is missing. Okay. So how did I get here? What happened to me? Someone must have brought me here, I didn't walk here on my own did I?"

The talker looked at me for a moment and said slowly. "You know, that's the funny thing about it."

Somehow I wasn't in a humorous mood but said it anyways. "So humor me."

"You were found a few hours after the kidnapping,..."

He'd said it outright. She'd been nabbed.

"...you know how all the traffic lights have cameras to film people going through the red lights? Well, they film all the people going through the yellow ones too. There's a picture of you racing through the light just before the incident occurred. You travel through the intersection, the camera records the kidnapping, but you don't return to the scene. We combed the entire area for a city block. Closed the whole place down for half the night to gather evidence. You were found a few hours later by some citizens after we'd already left. You and your bike looked as though you had crashed into an abandoned building down an alley, and gone un-noticed, and you were unconscious."

'Looked' like I had crashed into the building.

The talker apparently had nothing more to say, and now they both just sat there studying at me.

"We're in a bit of a pickle here..," said the talker.

You're telling me, I thought.

"...you see, we have to get some answers out of you fast. We, the agency of which you are an employee, is in a lot of trouble. You, personally are in it up to your neck."

They thought I was connected to the

operation somehow. I was screwed. "If there's been a kidnapping, and I'm the last person to see them, why aren't the police here asking me questions?"

The talker smiled. "Now that's pretty funny. I'll tell you what, why don't you just relax for a while. Get some rest, maybe an hour or two of sleep, and maybe your memory will come back to you, and we'll chat again, how about that?"

"Whatever you say." I closed my eyes and I could hear them get up and move towards the door.

They went outside and I heard the knob click closed. They were talking right outside the door but I couldn't make out what they were saying. I looked at the intravenous tube from the saline solution going into my arm. If only I could get rid of all this stuff I could listen by the door.

They were going to knock me out again with drugs, keep me under wraps for a while and come back and question me again. Maybe they'd give me sodium pentothal next time, or water board me. It wouldn't matter, I didn't know anything. As far as I knew anyways.

I closed my eyes to think. The elephant was sitting on my chest again and it was hard to breathe. Three broken ribs will do that to you. And then I remembered where I'd seen the silent suit. It was when I was first hired by the agency four years ago.

One of the new guys I was training with for the perimeter, he pointed this weird looking guy out to me on the gun range, firing a big handgun. He was a pretty good shot.

"See that guy over there? Don't look, just glance. I heard it through the grapevine that they call him the Eraser."

"What the hell does that mean?" I asked.

"If they ever have a problem, within the agency I mean, they send the Eraser in, and he erases it. I think when they say problem, they mean people."

Now I could remember that day very clearly, loading my hand gun with more rounds of bullets and looking under the brim of my hat at the guy. He was strange looking even back then, pale and thin with angular cheeks and nose.

"They should have named him pencil, look how skinny the guy is." I was fresh from Baghdad. "I'll go over there and kick his ass right now," I said. "And get this over with."

"Go ahead, but keep me out of it," said my new buddy. "I need this job."

With my eyes closed on the bed in the hospital, elephants sitting on my chest I wondered. Did they send the Eraser for me? I sure as hell was vulnerable right about now, and had messed up somehow, let the rich guy's friend get kidnapped while I had slept through the whole damn thing under mysterious circumstances.

Since I wasn't one to sit idly by, just waiting to get my ass kicked, or worse, and especially since I was currently in such a compromised situation, it seemed best to take matters into my own hands.

Hospital beds are kind of like tables at restaurants, and I reached under the bed and found some old chewed up gum someone had stashed and pulled a piece of it off. Then I unwrapped the bandage on the inside of my elbow and pulled out the intravenous needle, plunged it into the gum to plug it up, cleaned the excess off the needle and placed it back onto my arm laying it flat but not inserting it, this way with it plugged it wouldn't leak all over the place, and they'd never be the wiser that I wasn't getting whatever dose they were giving, then re-bandaged the whole set-up, just before the door opened again with the two suits and the doctor leading the way.

"We're just going to give you a little something to make you more comfortable and to help you sleep," said Dr. Evil.

I opened my eyes to slits. "Sure," I mumbled, and watched him measure out a syringe and insert it into the bag that was hanging over my arm.

They waited a couple of minutes in silence, watching me, my eyes opened to the tiniest of cracks and I could see their shadows, standing there. The doctor looked at his watch, then got out a tiny flashlight and opened my left eye lid and pointed the beam directly on my eyeball which I had rolled back and was keeping still.

"He's out," said the doctor.

The suits seemed satisfied and left the room with the drug pusher while I planned my next move. I figured that I had at the most a couple of hours to either get myself out of there standing up on my own two feet, or be taken out in a body bag.

3.

I hadn't been in a hospital since I'd gotten my tonsils out as a kid, and I'd forgotten how they were set up.

If I remembered correctly, the rooms all opened up onto a hallway and somewhere in the middle was a nurse's station where they monitored the heart rate machines that were hooked up to the patients. If I unhooked that contraption now, they would get the warning signal and come to check it out. I decided to test it out. I moved the tape off my chest near my heart and sure enough the box started beeping loudly. I could hear footsteps and closed my eyes. Through slits I could see the Eraser and the nurse looking down at me. She took one look and put the tape back in place and the beeping went back to normal.

"The tape just fell off," she said.

"How do you know he's not awake?" said the Eraser.

"Not a chance. We gave him enough to

knock out a horse. He's in lala land."

"Shine the light in his eyes, I want to see."

"Suit yourself." She opened my right eye with her fingers and shined a small flashlight at my eyeball which I had rolled up into my socket.

"Yeah, he looks pretty conked out," said the Eraser. "I guess if the tape falls off again I can just come in here and put it back. Give you a break, eh sweet stuff?"

She didn't seem too pleased with his advances.

"Um, sure whatever, I could use a break, it's been a long day, and we have to go through this whole charade again pretty soon."

Charade she'd said. This was all faked.

When they left the room, I sat up and looked around. I needed a weapon. They'd gone to a lot of trouble to make it look like a real hospital room. There was a phone, clock, radio, magazines, TV. I focused my attention on the phone. I'd never clocked anyone with a phone before, but I'd seen it done at a party once when I was in the gang. It broke the guys jaw like he'd used a bat. I unplugged the cable and the handset, and hefted it in my hand. It was kind of like a square bowling ball and I could grip it pretty tight.

I hid it under the blanket and practiced a couple of times and then undid the tape again. It'd only been a few minutes since they'd been in here, that should piss 'ol Eraser off pretty good. Sure enough he came in swearing under his breath, got close and I conked him upside the head, knocking him clean out and was able to catch him before he fell and made any noise.

I wheeled him around and laid him down in the bed, covered him with the blanket, attached the electrodes to his chest and the machine started beeping normally again. Then I pulled out the needle from my arm, broke it in half since the end was plugged with gum and found his vein and slipped it in and taped it up. Horse tranquilizer my eye.

"Let's see how you like it punk."

I cracked the door open just a smidgen and peeked out, and I'll be damned if it didn't look like a real hospital ward. There was a nurses station and a long row of other rooms open with beds and curtains drawn. But the place was empty, not a single soul was stirring. I could just walk to the stairway next to the elevator and make my escape.

I was still a little groggy and hadn't thought the whole thing all the way through, and I looked down at my bare feet. I was dressed in a patient gown and the back was open to the wind, naked on my backside. If I made it to the street, they'd arrest me for indecency.

I locked the door and looked in the closet by the bed for my clothes, but it was empty. So I stripped Eraser and put on his suit, and looked in the mirror and I'll be damned if we weren't about the same size, length wise anyways. He was thinner and I had to squeeze into the jacket and pants.

His clothes smelled like after shave cologne and I wondered if he put some in the wash to get them this way, or if it eroded off him as he sweated, and I made a mental note to get the hell out of these clothes as soon as I got the hell out of here.

The black shiny shoes were too small but they'd have to do, I wear a size thirteen and these were elevens at the most, so I tied them loose and curled my toes.

He had a Smith & Wesson .44 with a full clip of bullets in a shoulder holster and the mirrored pair of sunglasses in his vest and I slid them on and slicked back my hair and noticed the hospital wristband on my left wrist, broke it off and tossed it in the trash can at the corner of the door.

I looked closer in the mirror.

There's a raw scrape on my chin and another one that runs from the edge of my hairline down the right side of my face to my ear like I'd been dragged upside down on the asphalt. I looked like hell, but better than Eraser man at the moment I figured. I adjusted the sunglasses and smiled a crooked smile.

Good enough.

I opened the door a crack to peer out, and now there's a nurse sitting at the desk, the same one I'd seen in my room earlier. Dressed in a perfect white suit with flowing brown hair, Nurse Amber. She was writing on a pad of paper on the desk in front of her, and every now and then looking over at the clock on the wall. She was trouble and I'd have to get by her to get to the exit door.

Nothing could be done about it. Maybe she'd think I was Eraser and ignore me like she did when she was in the room with him. I waited for her to look down and start writing again and then made my move, opened the door slow and silky, and walked steadily for the exit, turning the scraped side of my face away from her and scratching the other side of my face while hiding my scraped chin with my hand.

On the edge of my vision I could see her look up as I passed and then look quickly back down at her desk as I pushed through the door. She hated the guy who she thought was me.

I was out.

The hallway is big enough for a small bus, bright with linoleum floors and an elevator bank twenty feet to the right with two doctors standing in front of it. They've pushed the top button, I can see it shining white. They're going up, and talking in low tones as they wait. Luckily they're not the two doctors that were in my room but I don't know who might be exiting the elevator that's on its way and I have to get out of here.

Walking steadily past the elevator bank I scratch my face and hide my scraped chin and explain myself with a murmur as I open the stairway door.

"I need the exercise."

The big number on the inside of the stairway wall says five, and I take the stairs down two at a time, any more than that and I'll fall flat on my head and wind up back at the hospital, probably for good.

I'm on the bottom floor now open the heavy metal fire door a crack to peer out. The stairwell ends up on the outside of the building which makes sense because it's a fire escape. I can't tell if it's morning or afternoon, but it's one of the two, the sun low in the horizon, east or west I had no idea. It's a dull orange haze probably half an hour before dark.

I move quickly to the other side of the building to get space between me and the exit door I just used. I need to get away from this place as fast as I can without attracting attention and I keep my feet moving. It's pretty busy outside, I'm near the parking lot and it's packed. I see people with different colored lab coats, walking here and there carrying papers, and folks in wheelchairs, there's the entrance to the ER on the corner. Cop cars and ambulances. What the hell do you know about that, this is a real hospital.

Two black SUVs race up to the building that I just exited, and out leap a bunch of guys in black suits. I crouch by some cars near the ER and watch them.

Half of them race into the building and the other half fan out around the building. The ones on the outside don't know what to do, I can tell they're not perimeter guys, they look around frantically at all the activity, cars coming and going, people everywhere, a lot of action, too much for them. They're even looking up at the building, looking at the windows like I might have rappelled out of one with a rope or bed sheets tied together. Maybe they think I'm spider man with suction cups on my hands jumping around up there.

The logo on the building says 'St. Jude'. The patron saint of lost causes. Figures.

I move like an alley cat between the cars, keeping low and putting distance between us. I'm at the ER now and can see in the entrance. There's two cops and they're holding a guy with cuffs between them at the window, checking him in. The guy with cuffs doesn't look too happy. That explains the cop cars. I pass them by and head to the ambulances.

Normally an ambulance would be a great getaway vehicle. No one wants to stop an ambulance to look for an escaped guy, just in case it was on a real emergency call, and you're the putz that made someone who's hurt lose out.

Unfortunately this one is facing towards the building I just left and if I'm the guy driving it, they'll spot me right away. I'm gonna use the bulk of it to shield me and then sprint to the other side of the building and get the hell away from this property. I run out of cars to crouch next to, and the ambulance is sitting at the perfect angle to hide me while I make my exit.

I'm thinking I'm pretty smart with my back on the side of the square ambulance when I spot two white shirted EMT guys running for the exit doors, heading for their vehicle. My goose is cooked. I check the back door of the ambulance. It's locked, so I slide underneath and wait till they unlock the front doors which should unlock all the doors.

While I'm under the EM truck I can see under the cars all the way to my old building. Black shoes are moving through the lot towards me, and I can see one of the guys is looking under the cars, so I scoot next to the big back tire and curl up. I hear the EMT's boots scuffle the rocky asphalt as they stop at their doors and make my move, slide quick onto the back bumper ledge, open one of the doors at the same moment they open theirs, and squeeze in quick as I can, close the door and roll under the gurney on the side. It's the kind with wheels that slide right up into the back of the ambulance and I wait in its shadow as the engine fires to life. Sirens wail and the truck lurches forward, lumbers over a gutter, onto the street, bouncing my head off the gurney, and takes off. I'm on my way. Where to, I have no idea.

I can tell this guy's a good driver, he doesn't stop or slow down, just wheels it from side to side, and it's taking all my energy to keep from sliding out from under the gurney. I've got both my feet wedged into the back wheels and have a death grip on the undercarriage of the contraption.

As we careened through the streets I considered my options. Number one I need to stay out of the clutches of the agency and especially pretty little nurses with needles. Not to mention the Eraser.

Number two I need to gather intelligence

quickly. Find out what happened. What in the hell happened. I don't have a number three yet.

The ambulance is slowing down. I peek out from the gurney and see the driver looking intently out the front of the windshield, looking for a place to park the truck. We're here. It's loud. There's an orange glow and a popping and crackling sound. Something bad is happening. There's more sirens all around, heading this way, people yelling, running, bullhorns.

I slide out from my hiding spot and out the door. It's chaos. There's a building on fire, hoses everywhere and water covering the street. The ambulance is parked far enough away to stay out of the danger zone, but close enough to hear the crackling of the flames, feel some of the heat and the burnt air, thick with smoke and ash swirling around me. It's a five story brick building fully engulfed in flames, flames jetting out of the windows, geysers of water from hoses raining down from every angle on the roof which collapses with a groan.

A policeman nearby spots me, pegs me as a civilian in my suit and tie, and yells at me.

"Are you injured?"

I shake my head no and he waves me towards a crowd of people on the side behind a yellow tape an barricades. I walk a few feet into the crowd and then quietly to the back perimeter and watch from the edge. It's comfortable here. I like it on the perimeter. I can see what's going on all around me now, and no one notices me taking it all in. I'm a spectator, like everyone else. Just like everyone else.

We're nearer the city than we were at the hospital, the tallest buildings loom over us in the background, shutting half the sky, gray and black monoliths with mirrored windows.

There's ten fire engines, five ambulances, over thirty cop cars and hundreds of people watching the scene from the edges. Three helicopters are hovering nearby, probably filming the action for the evening news. I can see the station logo on two of the copters. I feel a sense of calm while watching the scene of destruction and mayhem from my vantage point.

My ambulance drivers are just standing by their truck, talking with a policeman. They don't look concerned, their body language doesn't show anxiety, fear, anticipation. They don't seem to have noticed that I was in their truck, and they're not in a hurry to administer first aid to anyone. I watch the building engulfed in flames. There's scaffolding on the side, some of the windows are missing, there's a couple of large dumpsters next to the building, and there's no landscaping. It's a construction site. Someone probably threw a cigarette butt near some oil based paint and started the damn thing. The ambulance drivers are relaxed because no one is injured. All that crazy driving to get here just in case someone needed help, and now this.

My eyes and senses take in everything

around me. No one is watching me, monitoring me, looking at me with questions in their minds and eyes. I'm just a part of the crowd, anonymous and invisible.

I move away from the scene and walk slowly and methodically away from the action, I see everything around me, every movement, every person, every vehicle and window. No alarms are going off in my head. I pull out the slim wallet from the inside coat pocket, there's about a hundred in cash, some credit cards, and a driver's license, no ID marking the Eraser with the Agency, but the home address on the driver's license is the Agency's headquarters. His name is Jerry Adam Smith. Sure it is pal. Sure it is.

I pocket the cash, and kept walking with the wallet in my hand. No way was I going to throw it in a trash can or the mailbox, someone would find it too soon and be able to trace it to this location and check the video cameras and track my movements out of here so I stood next to a storm drain in the gutter, put the wallet inside my pants as though I was putting it in a pocket, then dropped it along my leg next to my shoe, looked around once to see if anyone was watching and kicked it in. Someone would find it someday, maybe it would end up on a river bank after a rainstorm, or wash out onto a beach, and hopefully by the time that happened this would all be settled.

I walked towards some cabs sitting idly by a coffee shop, the drivers watching the action back at the fire and picked out the one I wanted. A Middle Eastern looking guy. They don't talk. I got into the cab without a word and when he got in the driver's seat and turned to me I told him three words.

"Market and Vine." The old part of the downtown area. He drove without a word, which is what I wanted. Cabbies like this are smart, they've been around. I looked at his ID on the dashboard. He looked Iraqi, and his name looked Iraqi. Al-Bayati. I wanted to talk to him, ask him about his story, how he got here, what does he do besides drive a cab, how many kids does he have. The usual. But it wasn't the time or place. I kept my eyes forward watching where he was going, which route he was taking. He was good, not once did he look directly at me in the rear view mirror, but I could tell he was observing me in the corners of his eyes. He was wondering what my story was too. A guy dressed in a suit and tie with a military buzz cut getting in his cab and remaining silent must be giving him the jitters. Plus I just woke up from a coma, and looked like a walking corpse.

"This is fine," I called out to him and he pulled over by the corner of Market street. The fare meter read ten dollars and I handed him a ten and a five and got out without a word. A fifty percent tip. I knew that even if they had my picture on the evening news with a reward he wouldn't say a thing. Guys like this minded their own business, they'd been through enough trouble where they were from and were never looking for more of it, they were trying to stay the hell away from it.

As I walked I took off the jacket and the tie and rolled up my sleeves, it was getting hot, and I needed to jettison some clothes. There was a homeless man sitting in an alley next to a shopping cart full of his belongings and I laid the jacket and tie on top the cart and kept going.

A few doors down I went into a second hand store and bought a tie dye tee shirt and a Dodgers baseball hat, and kept moving. Around the corner I went into another second hand store and bought some pants and running shoes. Then I found another homeless guy and gave him the rest of Erasers clothes.

It seemed like the closer you got to the center of the city, the more homeless and second hand stores you found, and when you at the very epicenter of the city, they disappeared. It was as though the hub was reserved for the ultra-hip and rich, while the outskirts were ringed with despair, and hopelessness.

I kept walking towards the city, I needed the exercise, needed to clear my brain. I still had a splitting headache and my side ached with broken ribs. I'd walk the pain away.

The sun is setting and there's a golden glow enveloping the skyline, while in the midst of the tall buildings, the shadows are deepening.

I keep an apartment and a car in the city, in separate buildings separated by a few city blocks. The apartment's out of the question, too many people know about it, and they'll have someone there, waiting, watching. The car however, is in a an obscure location and no one knows about it. Tucked into a public lot on the second floor of an office building. That's my destination. The car has false floorboards and a few choice weapons and night vision gear.

"Hey man, where you go'in'?" A voice rings out nearby. A gang of rough looking punks has taken up residence at a corner near a liquor store on my path. I think about heading to the other side of the street, but there's another gang of punks over there too. It's getting near night time and the rats are coming out of the sewers. The tall gangly one is looking at me and shouts again.

"I sayeed, hey man where you go'in?"

As though I didn't hear him the first time.

He steps in front of me, blocking my way. I can't afford any trouble right now but it's standing right in front of me.

He's a spindly mulatto, part white, part Latino and part black, while the gang he's running with is mostly black with a couple of white guys thrown in for good measure. An equal opportunity gang. He's either trying to prove something to the guy who's running this pack, or he's the guy running the pack trying to prove something to his troops. Either way he's trying to prove something, and at that moment in time, I was it.

From far away in the fading light I probably looked like a hippy or a big kid from the suburbs in a goofy tie dye shirt and running shoes. Someone harmless and easily pushed around.

Now that I'm closer to him he can tell that I'm packing some weight, but it's the opposite of fat and he can see the serious look in my eyes and it makes him hesitate, I can see that he wants to move away from me, get some space between us, but now that he's started this whole thing he can't back down too quickly or he'll lose respect from the pack of hyenas.

I'm just one guy, and they are many. He speaks lower now, as the others watch him from the side, talking just loud enough for me and him to hear it.

"Say homey, you lost? You need directions or somethin', I only charge five dollah."

All I want right now is to just get by him, but there is no way in hell that I'm gonna give this jive turkey five bucks to walk down a public street. My head hurts and my ribs ache and the last thing I need is to get into a fistfight with this pencil neck. I lift my shirt like I'm going to reach into my pocket for the money, lift it just enough to show him the handle of the gun, while I keep watching him.

He laughed. "Hey, I got one of those too, check this out." And he lifted his shirt to show me his gun. "We all got one."

He looks from the gun and back up at my face again and sees a seriousness that he didn't expect when he called me out a few moments ago. I don't give a damn if he and his pals have guns. He can tell by my eyes that I've actually used a gun before, and I'll use this one on him and all his buddies right now if I have to. He squinted in the darkening light at me, looking at my eyes. "What are you man, part Indian?"

I kept my eyes on him waiting for him to make a move and answered. "I'm part nothin'... man."

He nodded while he thought this over, then bit his lip and stepped back and motioned with an open hand for me to continue on my journey. I waited till the gang opened a lane wide enough for me to get through without having to push my way against them. When I was far enough away he called out to me again.

"Alright, alright! You don't say much, but you know the magic word, go in peace brothah!"

The magic word around these parts is handgun.

I decided to do something about my headache and stopped into a convenience store for some aspirin and a coffee, and while I'm paying for it I check out the date on the newspapers in the rack next to the cashier. There's no mention of the star being kidnapped. I looked at the front page then flipped all the way to the fifth pages, nothing. The date on all the papers say the fourteenth. Now how in the hell can it be the fourteenth today if we'd escorted the star on the night of the thirteenth, and I'd been in coma as the good doctor had said, for 'a couple of days'?

I knew without a doubt that we'd escorted the star on the thirteenth because some of the other guys were worried that it was a bad luck day and I told them it was hogwash. "The thirteenth is a good a day as any," I told them. "Probably better than any other since most people are afraid of it and you can get the jump on them." Prophetic words.

"Are these newspapers a day old?" I asked the guy behind the register.

"If you mean by a day old are they today's papers, yes. They brought them here this morning."

"Then today's the fourteenth?"

"All day and half the night," he said with a grin.

Wise guy. I paid for my aspirin and coffee and went back outside. It was darkening quick now, and the lights of the city were taking over the skyline.

We'd made our move escorting the star right before midnight of the thirteenth, and now it was around six at night on the fourteenth. It had been eighteen hours since they hit us. I'd been awake for about two hours, and out like a light for sixteen hours. A lot can happen in sixteen hours.

I kept on my walking journey to the city, the skyscrapers getting closer. I cut down a side alley between blocks, past a tattoo parlor and a pool hall and came out on Halo street, a heck of a name for a street with all the trouble lurking in the shadows.

My car was parked on the second floor of the building across the street and I stayed in the darkness of the alley and watched for a while. The street was busy, lots of cars going each way, people on the sidewalks heading home or to work or out to eat, a few drunks staggering from bar to bar, the usual. It was crowded and I liked crowds. A police cruiser went slowly by and I melded into the brick wall.

I saw a bunch of revelers exit a restaurant and getting ready to head across the street and I joined them, sticking close behind as they made their way across the road. Like I was part of their group, part of the fun. They were laughing and telling jokes while they walked and had obviously been drinking, probably all day by the looks of it. They were boisterous and loud. They didn't notice me trailing them, and when we got to the other side of the street, they went one way, and I went the other.

I like this particular parking garage because it's busy, there's always a lot of cars going in and out, and it's easy to get lost in the shuffle. It's on the edge of the red light district and one of many restaurant rows in the shadow of the city.

I walked next to the overhang of the building blending into the side of it, maneuvering through the crowd, keeping my eyes ahead, not focused on any one particular thing, but everything. Looking for anything that stands out. Watching for the watchers.

There's a side entrance on the alley that not many people know about, and I go quickly through the door and start up the stairs. There's a light out on the second floor landing and it's dark. I wait for my eyes to get used to the darkness. This is the type of thing most civilians need to be aware of, a light out in a stairway could mean a mugger is waiting in the shadows to do some mugging and I go up the stairs cautiously. I have the gun in my hand and ready, and if there's a mugger he's gonna get the surprise of his life, but it's clear, and when I get to the second floor landing, the light flickers on and then off again. A malfunction, that's all.

Car tires squeal as they maneuver up the circular corkscrew drive up through the vertical parking lot, and I see my little blue sedan parked in the middle of the lot. I stay in the shadow of the stairwell, thankful for the malfunctioning light and watch and wait.

I stay there for the next twenty minutes or so, and watch as people come off the elevator and pick up their cars, or park their cars and get into the elevator. I watch their eyes and their body language. I use them like crickets in the night while on the perimeter. Normally if a person sees someone lurking in a car or in a corner or a shadow they'll look that way, and I watch to see if they are startled by anyone else on the second floor parking lot. I only use the car to stash equipment and I haven't taken it out of the lot since I put here six months ago. No one knows about it. But still... Old habits die hard. I watch.

A couple of guys in their mid-twenties with curly black hair and little beards get out of the elevator, talking and joking and then split up and walk around the cars, looking in each one of them, casing the place. They're up to no good, that's easy enough to see. Looking to boost a car and go for a joy ride, or just rifle through them looking for cash or anything else they can find. Most of the cars up here are late model cars, most of them have alarms, tough to jack. Mine is about the oldest one here. Unfortunately. They've just about finished their rounds, and it looks like they've focused on my car, and I really wish they would just go away. They're talking about it over the top of my car while they have it surrounded. The shorter guy is on the driver's side while his cohort is on the passenger side and they look like they're still undecided. Maybe they'll talk themselves out of it I'm thinking and I won't have to hurt them. If they do decide to break into my car I'll make sure they regret it.

Suddenly, the shorter guy on the driver side pulls a slim Jim from his pants and slides it through the crack in the door and unlocks it and pulls on the handle. The sound of the deep thud and the shock wave compresses the meat on my face and arms as the car explodes in a ball of flame and I half scramble half dive into the stairwell to escape the shrapnel of metal and body parts that's peppering the walls with sickening splatters. The echo of the blast reverberates in the concrete structure back and forth against the walls ringing in my eardrums, what's left of them.

Someone booby trapped my car that no one was supposed to know about. They'll find out soon enough that it wasn't me they got, I don't have curly black hair.

The seismic action sets off a hundred car alarms on every floor of the parking facility. I run down the stairway with a pack of other people frantically escaping, and exit the alley door calmly and don't look back. I blend into the crowd that's forming nearby and count my blessings. Those bastard car thieves just saved my life.

Another car explodes, and then another, and a fireball erupts out of the openings in the building. My exploding car is starting a chain reaction with all the other cars next to. Gas tanks are heating up and blowing up. People stop watching and start running for their lives away from the area. The fire department is going to be pretty busy tonight.

I walk quickly back the way I came, through the alley back to Market street. Someone rigged my car, it looked like C-4 explosives, and a basic trigger on the driver's side handle. I'd heard about this kind of thing before, never actually seen it in action though. It's the kind of extreme method the mob and the CIA used to eliminate people.

There's no going forward for now, I have to figure this out. They rigged my car, they probably rigged my apartment, whoever they are, they'd probably blow me up when I opened the front door. There's no reason to go anywhere near my apartment, it was my known place of residence. They'll have surveillance on it and won't pull them off until they have me back in custody. I need quick answers. There's absolutely no reason to go forward until I gather some facts. I need to backtrack. But first I needed to consider my options. I could either disappear completely and go underground, I could go to the police, or I could go to the agency. If I disappeared they'd find me someday, they always do, and my dream of running my own security firm and having a happy life would be over, I'd be living under a rock for the rest of my life and wondering what happened. If I went to the police they'd put me in a cell where I'd be an easy target. If I went to the agency they'd put me to sleep again, maybe this time for good. But there was a fourth option, I could go underground and , but I was on my own.

I flagged a cab down. It was an old guy driving, chain smoker, thin and wrinkled. "Where to pal?" he asked me with a hoarse voice.

"St. Jude's hospital."

"Which one?"

I hadn't thought of that. When I'd flown the coop I hadn't looked at the street names, I was hiding under a gurney in an ambulance. But I remembered the direction we'd travelled. "Straight south, five miles."

"Bell and Figueroa."

"That's the one." I had no idea if that was in fact the one, but I'd know when I got there.

When we got to the cross street before the hospital I could tell it was the same St. Jude's that I'd escaped from a couple of hours ago. There was the tower of rooms on the side and the parking lot and the ER building on the other end with ambulances parked in front ready to go.

"This is fine," I told the cabbie and gave him a twenty for the fifteen dollar ride. Another big tip from the Eraser.

The area around the hospital was mostly homes and apartment buildings and I walked casually. Just another guy out for some exercise in the early evening. I passed by a car parked on the side and could see the clock lit up on the dashboard. Eight o'clock. They probably had a visiting time schedule at the hospital, and I imagined eight o'clock was right around that time. There was a bus stop on the corner across from St. Jude's and I found a spot in the shadow of a tree and leaned against the trunk, blending into it.

They wouldn't expect me to come back to the hospital. There's no way they'd be prepared for it. I scanned the fifth floor windows, some lights were on, but they were all covered with drapes, no help there. People were coming and going through the front door, mostly leaving.

Visiting time was over.

I didn't really have a plan, but I figured if I got back into the hospital I could search the fifth floor and maybe find something, anything. Maybe run into one of the agency guys, or that Asian doctor with the big fingers and pump him with sodium pentothal and get some answers out of him.

There's a security guy at the front, a regular guy with a standard uniform, rent-a-cop badge, white shirt and black tie, milling around, talking into his phone.

I spotted some nurses leaving the side door of the building, bunched up together, saying their goodbyes as girls often do, hugging and laughing, and then heading in different directions in the parking lot. One of the nurses is my nurse. Amber. I can tell it's her even from this distance the way she's busting out in all the right places. She's headed to a far corner of the parking lot, near my bus stop. I need to interview my first witness.

It's a little too bright, too many lights in the parking lot but there's no way around it, I'm on a tight time schedule. I hustle across the street as a bus goes by, using it as a shield. The sidewalk borders the lot and her car is parked right up against a hedge. She sees me and smiles, just a big kid or a young hippy in a baseball cap and tie dye shirt, it's funny how this type of shirt always triggers a mellow reaction in people. They think that because you're wearing it you must be mellow or stoned to the eyeballs and harmless. And then she recognizes my face. "Oh!" Her cheeks turned red.

I showed her the gun and motioned for her to get in the car. "I'm not going to hurt you, I just want some answers." I could see the security guy still talking on the phone, looking at his feet. Worthless piece of garbage. She got in the car and I squeezed in the seat behind her.

"Remember me?"

"Room five A."

"That's right, you have a good memory. It must be tough remembering everyone that comes in and out of that hospital."

"You said you wouldn't hurt me."

"And I won't. Just answer some questions simple as that. So you do recognize me."

"I recognize your face, but as for the rest, you're wearing clothes now, it's hard to tell."

"What?"

"I'm a nurse, it's no big deal. It's part of the job. It's kind of like washing a car after a while. When they brought you in last night you were one big scrape from head to toe. I gave you a sponge bath and bandaged you up."

Now my cheeks turned red. "When they brought me in?"

"Yeah, the guy's in the suit and ties. They cleared out a whole floor for you, said it was a national emergency. They sure were angry when you walked out, especially the guy you put in your place with the broken needle. I think he's got a grudge against you now."

"So you really are a nurse?"

"I just got off an eighteen hour shift and I'm tired okay? My feet are tired, my brain is exhausted from all the action today and I just want to go to bed."

She saw my eyebrows raise up in the rear view mirror and shook her head. "That's not what I meant. Now are you going to ask your questions or not?"

I was speechless for a moment, thinking.

"Look," she said. "If the security guard

doesn't see me drive away soon, he'll come to check on me. You better hurry up." She started the car and put it in reverse. "I'll give you a ride out of here okay? Just duck down on the seat till we get clear."

I crouched down on the back seat and watched her as she drove, backing up and going forward, turning out of the lot into traffic. She kept her eyes forward, didn't wave at anyone or make any gesture.

Maybe not making a gesture was in itself making a gesture. That was paranoid thinking and I re-routed my train of thought. I was feeling weak and tired. When it seemed that we were far enough away I sat back up. Just that little move made the blood leave my head and I got woozy and closed my eyes.

She was watching me in the rear view mirror.

"When's the last time you ate?"

"I had an aspirin and a cup of coffee a couple of hours ago, why?"

"You need food."

"I need answers."

"First you need food. I'm a nurse, I know what you need, trust me. You'll go into hypoglycemic shock without some fat, protein and carbohydrates soon." She pulled into a fast food drive through and ordered two burgers and a soda. "Health food," she said as she drove forward to the window.

I pulled out a twenty and handed it to her. "My treat." Actually it was the Erasers treat but who was keeping track.

I wolfed down the burgers and slurped the soda while she pulled back onto the highway, and I began to feel whole again. I hadn't really noticed her car. It was a heap, clean but old.

"They don't pay you very much as a nurse do they?"

"Are you kidding me? I get by, but that's about it. That's all I really need though, for now, to get by."

"Isn't there a Mr. nurse?"

"Used to be. He used to joke all the time that he was going to upgrade to a younger model, and then one day he did."

"Can't believe you'll be single long."

"How about a year?"

I whistled. "You must be joking."

"I don't joke, and I don't lie. I hate liars, and I hate what happened back at the hospital. They were lying to you about being in a coma for a couple of days."

"I know. I found out when I looked at today's date on a newspaper."

She eyed me in the rear view mirror. "You don't look like a liar. You're not are you?"

I took my time and shook my head. "Not if I can help it. There's always those situations where lying might help someone avoid feeling stepped on, or hurt. I could have told you this is the nicest car I've ever been in, but I didn't."

"You didn't say it's the worst you've ever been in either."

"Tell me about the hospital, how long have you worked there?"

"Three years."

"Why'd they bring me there?"

"I don't know. We got the call from the top. Clear a floor quick, it was pretty tough. And then you showed up."

"Who brought me there?"

"The same guys who were there when you woke up, plus a few more that looked the same. Young, military looking, suits. Serious. You were unconscious, and pretty ragged. Like I said, we cleaned you up, they took some blood samples and x-rays, and we bandaged you up. Then we had a little meeting where they told us how to act. I was there when the doctor got the toxicology report. You were high on drugs."

"I don't take drugs. I don't even drink."

"That's what I thought by looking at you. I see druggies at the hospital all the time. You didn't fit the bill. Not willingly anyways."

"Someone drugged me before they brought me there, I was riding a motorcycle, something hit me, I blacked out, I don't remember what happened. What'd they use to bring me out of my fake coma?"

"Adrenaline. It counters the opiates."

"What happened when I left the building?"

"They came and got me, questioned me."

"The same guys who were in the hospital room?"

"A lot of different ones. But they all looked the same." She looked at me in the mirror. "They yelled at me."

"Yeah, well I owe you. My names Badger Thompson."

She glanced again in the mirror. "You're

named after an animal?"

"I get that a lot. Sort of a family tradition."

"Amber Clark." She pulled into an apartment complex, and parked in a marked stall. She pulled her purse off the seat, opened it and handed him her wallet. "Check my ID."

"That's okay. I don't need to..." I tried to push the wallet away but she was insistent.

"No, I want you to. Please."

I unlatched it. There was cash, coins, credit cards, driver's license, hospital ID. I flipped through them all. They all said Amber Clark. I was doing this for her sake. I'd already made up my mind about her. In my line of work you need to instinctively know when a person is telling the truth, and know it immediately. I could tell she was on the up and up when I came out of my coma. Even when she said the whole thing was a charade I knew she wasn't a part of it, didn't seem to like it. I carefully put everything back in place and handed her the wallet. I needed to move on.

"Alright, you check out. Thanks for the ride and the information." I got out of the car and opened the door for her and turned to leave.

"Do you want to come up for a cup of coffee?"

I turned back slowly.

She shrugged her shoulders. "It's easy to make."

"I just held you up with a gun, gave you the third degree."

"I've had worse done to me. Don't forget,

my husband left me for a younger woman. It doesn't get much worse than that."

"You haven't been around."

"Look, do you want the coffee or not?"

"Alright, one cup." I was feeling groggy again. Maybe it was the head injury, or the lingering effects of the drugs they and whoever else had given me, or maybe it was just the greasy burger slowing me down, clogging up my arteries. A cup of coffee sounded like the ticket right about now. I had a lot of ground to cover before daylight.

I followed her up the stairs and into the little apartment. It was like her car, old but clean, a one bedroom one bath rental with Formica on the floor and counters.

"Nice place," I lied.

She gave me a look that said, nice try. "Where'd you get that shirt?"

I looked down at the tie dye hippie shirt, the circle of colors radiating out from the center like an eyeball. There was a new color now, ketchup from the burger, and I wiped it with the back of my hand. "Whoops."

She went over to a box by the door and rummaged through it and pulled out a black tee shirt and black sweater and threw them towards me.

"This color works better at night."

"Your husbands' old clothes?"

"Are you kidding me? They all went in the trash last year. These are just some of my Dad's old clothes. He was about your size. I moved in here about a month ago and brought some old stuff with me, been meaning to take it to the second hand store."

"I do a lot of my shopping there."

She frowned. "Make yourself comfortable," she said and motioned to the couch and turned on the kitchen light. "I'll make that coffee."

I sat down in the couch and nearly got swallowed by the cushions. It was soft as a fluffy cloud. I thought about changing out of the hippy shirt and into the black tee shirt and sweater but my chin kept hitting my chest, and my eyes felt heavy like they were weighed down with bags of sand, fought to keep them open...

4.

In the Penthouse at the apex of the tallest building in the state the butler pulled the drapes back and spread out before them as far as the eye could see, the lights of the city and the surrounding suburbia sparkled and twinkled, multifaceted, multicolored, as though they were sitting on top of a giant diamond cut from a black rough. The windows themselves were fifteen feet high, the outsides tinted green like money and there really wasn't any need for drapes. They were mostly for show, like opening up the drapes that covered the screen in the old movie theatres. The butler tied them off with black ropes, then bowed to the man seated at the long desk.

Charles H. Washington II balanced a gold lighter on his thumb. His name was long and official and sounded like he was filthy rich, which he was, but his friends all called him C.W., or C-Dub for short which he liked since it sounded more like a rapper from the streets.

A medium built man, dark and brooding forehead with deep set eyes, sharp chin and nose, receding hairline with a tinge of gray, not yet forty and yet aging like he was well into his sixties, his face at any rate was aging. The stress of running a growing empire cracking the area around his eyes.

His body though was lean and strong like a middleweight boxer in the middle of training, the veins and sinews in his forearms popping as he raised a big cigar to his lips, took one puff and exhaled a cloud while taking in the city skyline.

"They're waiting sir," said the butler. It was more of an announcement than a reminder, and the butler stood silent on the side.

"Good, they can wait." And he smiled a crooked smile, his gold implants shining and took another puff on the cigar. It was the most expensive one you could buy, from a private garden in the countryside south of Havana. Yes, they can wait, he thought, like I waited all these years for just this moment in time, planning, scheming, killing even when needed...

Yes, everything was lining up nicely. The bid for the skyscraper was nearly complete, and a thousand luxury condos would soon be on the market, the residential development was moving forward, the golf course resort and casino were pumping cash, the record deals, the pro basketball team...

Now that would be the capper, forget about

the money involved buying it and pumping into it like a car at a gas pump.

To be able to sit on the sidelines and have everyone look at him and say, "That's the man" and be able to look right back at them in the eye and say "that's right, I am THE man now."

All these punk ass pro sports player wannabes looking for 'street cred' as they called it. He laughed at that. Hell, he wasn't only a product of the streets, from the streets, toughened by the streets, whatever you wanted to call it, he was actually born *on* the street, his Momma rest her soul giving birth to him on the asphalt black top on a hot summer night in Chinatown while she waited for the pimp that was in charge of her to bring a hit of ice so she could keep working through the night. Bring her the hit of ice that would kill her and bring him into this cruel world. And when he was old enough to learn the truth and learn the ropes, he vowed *never* to be that helpless again. He was never going to be laid out on the asphalt again, never.

He started out with one small grimy little tattoo shop in the inner city, about as big as a closet, and built that into one of the biggest companies in the country.

With foresight and providence, a man can do a lot with the few years he has allocated to him in this world. He was proof positive. When he heard the kid rapping away at the little tattoo shop, and the kid told him he didn't have a record contract, didn't even know what that meant, it's like a halo appeared over his head, like an angel sent to him from above delivering him from the pit, and the proceeds from the tattoo shop went into producing the first of many hit records, which only led to more opportunities. The night clubs, the record company, the real estate deals. Money was pouring in from all angles.

When you have cash money to spend and invest, the world is your cherry, and you'd best do well by cherry picking carefully. Sure there was a gun or two in the beginning, when things were panning out, people wouldn't cooperate, got in the way, and so those people disappeared here and there, now and then, it was all just part of the business, and it was always about the big picture, about rising from the dirt and grime and into the heavenly heights of respectability, and now he was legit, with the chief of police, the head of the biggest news outlet in the city, and the owner of the largest personal security company waiting for him in the outer office.

Waiting for him to call them all in.

The phone on the desk lit up and C-Dub reached for it. "Yes."

The voice on the other end was brief. "Production is going smooth, we have half a million CD's printed, and on their way to the outlets. Electronic download versions are ready to launch tomorrow morning, right on schedule."

"There's a been a problem. I think we need to postpone the release."

There was silence on the other end and C-

Dub could hear a panicked gasp for breath, as though he was choking on a piece of gristle. "Why, what's wrong?"

"I can't give you all the details. I just think it might be a good idea to delay the release date by a couple of days."

"C-Dub we've been pushing this as fast as possible to make the deadline. Orders have been filled, people have been paid. Every DJ in the country has it on their playlist for tomorrow morning. There's a lot of money, and a lot of our *reputation* on the line. We've shipped the product, and it's out there right now in the real world, and you know what that means. Bootleg copies are sure to hit the internet any minute. Someone somewhere has got their hands on it and is copying the album as we speak and printing it up in Asia, trying to get the jump on us. You postpone the release now and we'll be toast."

"I hadn't thought about that."

"Unless Gale died or something we need to stay on track and release this album tomorrow as planned. She didn't die did she?" His voice trailed off.

"No, she didn't die, as far as I know anyways. But I can't keep track of her every minute of the day. I have other things besides singers and albums to worry about."

"So what's the problem?"

"I might as well tell you now, since word is going to get out real soon. Gale's been kidnapped."

"Son of a bitch , what the hell happened?"

"I don't know yet, not everything anyways, just bits and pieces. She was headed to one of my clubs last night for a little pre-release party, no big deal, just show up, sing a few songs, meet a few fans and let off some steam. Everything was under the radar. No press release, no fanfare, just a little unwind time before she hit the talk shows in New York. On the way to the club someone whacked her security team and took her. We've been keeping it secret, waiting for the kidnappers demands."

"Nothing yet?"

"Nothing, that's why I thought it might be best to hold off on the release."

"Can't be done C-Dub. It's too late. It's too damn late. What the hell is wrong with this world?"

"Right now it's pretty messed up. Alright, go ahead and keep the presses going, we'll ride it out the best we can. I'll let you know as soon as we get any word."

C-Dub and put the phone back in the cradle and took another puff of the cigar. This album release was a microcosm of the world in general. No matter what disaster hit, the world kept spinning, life kept going on and on, and nothing could stop it.

The record was just one more piece of a giant puzzle fitting into place. His record company was launching Gale Nighting's new album, the one she'd been recording for the past few months and it was finally ready for release. It had taken too long, been too drawn out, too expensive and he had to put some heat on the production team to get it finished. They listened. Timing being the most important aspect of the entertainment industry, many would question the prudence of releasing it now that Nightingale was kidnapped, but there was nothing that could be done about it. The wheels of the bus were turning, and you either rode on top of it, or got run over by it.

"Alright Winston," he said as he put out the cigar in a gold tray. "Tell them I'll see them now."

He stood and greeted the men as they walked into the office, and motioned for them to sit opposite him, while the butler closed the giant doors and left the room. All three were in a somber mood, and their faces were hardened with remorse at recent events. There was Cole Garner, head honcho at network news, Blaine Thomas, Chief of Police for the city of Los Angeles, and Mason Takegawa, CEO and owner of the personal security agency in charge of protecting Nightingale when she was kidnapped.

The man sitting on the big chair tapped his fingers together, waiting for his guests to settle in their chairs.

The police chief spoke first.

"They want gold. We just got the call about an hour ago. They want ten gold bars, ten good delivery gold bars with four nines."

"That's a little steep don't you think? For a girl who's not yet a bonafide superstar?"

"What the hell is a good delivery bar?"

asked Cole. "And what the hell does four nines mean?"

"It's the type of gold that used in International bank transfers," said C-Dub. "A good delivery bar weighs four hundred ounces, and the four nines means they want it nearly pure."

"What about it," asked the Chief. "Can you get it together?"

"Gold is an amazing thing isn't it?" said C-Dub. "Untraceable currency, you can melt it down and do anything with it, buy anything. Buy anything except for love or so they say, and I'm not so sure about that. Empires are won and lost in the pursuit of it, entire generations destroyed for a piece of shiny metal from out of the dirt. It won't be easy to gather up that much pure gold, but I'll get it."

He got out a calculator and punched in some numbers. "A standard good delivery gold bar is four hundred ounces or twenty five pounds. They want ten bars, that's four thousand ounces and with today's gold price of thirteen hundred an ounce it comes to five point two million. Two hundred and fifty pounds. It'll fit in a small suitcase. When do they want it?"

"Tomorrow," said the Chief.

C-Dub threw the calculator on the table. "What, are they crazy?"

"Obviously. They kidnapped your girlfriend in the middle of the street in your city. I'd say they're insane."

"They think you'll pay it, mostly to keep it

out of the news."

"How do we know they're the ones who really pulled it off?"

"They gave us a couple of key details of the kidnapping, plus they left a card in the limo that was carrying Nightingale. The card had a code with numbers and letters so we'd know they were the kidnappers. I've never heard of something like this C-Dub, these guys are pretty thorough."

"Have there been any leaks yet Cole?"

"You told us to keep it under wraps, and so we have. There's nothing in the papers or on-line, not a trace. My guys are under strict orders. You know how this thing works though, someone will leak it soon enough, for a bit of cash."

"They'll never get away with it." He looked directly at the next chair, the head of the agency in charge of the protection. "What about your guy, the one they found in the building?"

Mason took a deep breath. "He got away."

"What the *hell* do you mean he got away?"

"He escaped. About twenty minutes ago. I had my number one team on it, they had him secured. We had him in a hospital, he was injured, they cleaned him up, drugged him up and were about to interrogate him when he escaped."

"What does he know?"

"Like I said, he escaped before they had a chance to interrogate him."

"I'm not asking *them* what he knows, I'm

asking *you.*"

Mason swallowed hard, his throat suddenly dry. He loosened the tie and unbuttoned the top button of his starched white shirt. "He was our perimeter guy, we found him a block away from the scene a couple of hours after the incident. I don't think he knows anything, he was probably too far away to see much."

" We've got an all-points bulletin out for him," said the chief. "I've got a thousand eyes looking for him all over this city."

"Find him Blaine. In the meantime what about the ransom? I don't have that kind of cash sitting around. I'll have to move some investments, cash in some loans."

"They said they'd call tomorrow with more instructions, they said they only want to talk with me," said the Chief. "Said they'd call me direct."

"That's fine. What's your contingency plan? In case the money doesn't work."

The chief was slow in response, he unfolded his hands and placed them on the table. "The money hardly ever works, in situations like this. I have to call in the FBI C-Dub, it's protocol for these cases. I know you don't want them to get involved, but..."

"Do what you gotta do," he replied. "Just get her back alive and in one piece. Alright gentlemen, let's all get on the same page. Blaine, call the FBI and get them in on the case. Cole, fire up the media, create a storm out of this story, let's put some heat on these guys who took Gale, maybe we can flush 'em out.

Mason, work with the chief on finding this perimeter guy of yours, what's his name?"

"Badger. Badger Thompson."

"Badger, you mean like an animal?"

"He's part Indian, his Dad was a quarter Comanche. It's sort of a tradition with some of these people, naming their kids after tough animals. He was in Iraq with the U.S. Army, did pretty good over there, showed that he could handle himself, so we picked him up when he got out. He was one of the best we had."

"Was one of the best you had," said C-Dub. I think maybe he had something to do with this whole thing, don't you? Why else would he run. My advice is to get a hold of that guy and maybe you'll be able to find Gale."

"I'm not so sure. It doesn't make sense. If he was part of the kidnapping, he would have gotten away from the scene with the kidnappers. But he was unconscious with injuries that were completely consistent with crashing his motorcycle into a building."

"There's something else," Mason continued. "We knew he had a car in the city, we got an inside tip so we sent a team to its location and when they got there the entire parking garage was blowing up."

"That was your guy?" asked the police chief. "He's a walking disaster area. I got a text about an hour ago. Fifty cars burned to a crisp and an entire city block evacuated. All I gotta say is you better find him before we do."

Mason looked hard at the police chief. "If

we find him first you'll never even hear about it."

"One more important item," said C-Dub. "Unfortunately, my record company is set to release Gale's new album tomorrow morning and there's nothing we can do to delay it. I know it's poor timing but I've been advised that if we don't release it as scheduled, someone else will."

Cole scrunched his face. "What do you mean someone else will?"

"Bootleggers," said C-Dub. "The album's been shipped around the world. It's either us or them and I'd rather have it be us."

"It's gonna look bad," said Cole. "Our newspaper reporting that she's been kidnapped while you're releasing a new album. It's gonna look like a scam."

"I've got an idea," said the Chief. "We'll have a news conference. We'll set it up official, have it in a good location, make sure all the news outlets are there. We'll present the facts, get it all out in the open. We're going to have to do it anyways so we might as well do it now and get it over with." He turned to Cole. "Make sure you get a couple of your guys in there, and make sure they're right up front to ask the right questions. I don't want this thing to get out of control, I hate news conferences. Damned reporters."

5.

Before I realized that I was sleeping and dreaming, I was walking through the desert, the sun setting on the horizon, a cool breeze on my face, tumbleweeds rolling by and I held out my hand and touched one as it went by.

My bare feet kicked up dust as I walked and when I looked behind me the scene looked dim and dark with roiling gray clouds, swirling over the distant mountains, lightning flickering.

A storm was gathering, but it was still far away. There was an arroyo up ahead, a small canyon with water, cool clear liquid, I could hear it gently bubbling over the round rocks, soothing and soft flowing life giving water.

I was thirsty, my throat dry and parched and I started down the gently rolling side of the arroyo towards the water at the bottom. It was beautiful and I smiled, it flowed from one end of the horizon to the other and seemed to have no end. I would drink from it and soothe my thirst.

My hand glanced against a rock as I climbed down the suddenly steep cliff and as I looked down at my hands I realized that I was dreaming, in that split second when you are straddling the fence between reality and dream I was in both worlds at the same time and wasn't sure which one I would wish to stay in, and then I heard the bacon in the pan, smelled the coffee, the thick aroma wafting in my nose and I opened my eyes.

I was laying on the couch in the living room of a friend, that much I hoped. A dull gray light filled the windows, it was dawn, that much I guessed.

And then the pain in my ribs reminded me in a heartbeat what transpired the night before, and I scanned the room with wide open eyes, I was on the run, that much I knew.

She was in the kitchen, her dark hair tied in a ponytail, dressed in a nurses uniform, a light blue one, the one she was wearing last night was white, that much I remembered. She was turning the bacon, flipping the eggs, the toaster made a mechanical popping sound and when she reached for it she looked over at me and smiled when she saw me looking at her.

"You forgot to drink your coffee last night, so I made a fresh pot."

I sat up and rubbed my eyes and tried to smile back. Was this a dream? No. Was I sure? I blinked and rubbed my eyes again and yawned and stretched, and then winced as my ribs separated. No, this wasn't a dream. "Did I sleep?"

"Like a log that snores. Are you hungry?"

My growling stomach answered that question and she laughed at the sound.

"What time is it?"

"Six AM. I have to go to work. You're welcome to stay here as long as you want. There's food in the fridge, a TV, and I even have a computer with internet if you want."

Six AM. I'd slept all night. She brought a plate with bacon, eggs, and toast and set it on the coffee table in front of me, then went back into the kitchen for the coffee.

"Cream or sugar?" she asked.

"Black," I said as I looked down at the plate of food and had to hold myself back from devouring it in one bite. "Are you eating?" I asked and waited for her reply.

She smiled as she set the steaming cup of coffee next to the plate. Her hair smelled like fresh strawberries, the same scent from the night before when I first saw her in the hospital, and I thought that must be one hell of a shampoo. Maybe it wasn't even the shampoo, maybe it was just her. She sat down in chair on the other side of the room and watched me. She was just sitting there smiling and I was a little puzzled, maybe she hadn't heard me the first time, so I asked her again. "Are you going to eat?"

She just giggled and shook her head. "In a minute, you go ahead."

I certainly didn't need to be asked twice and slowly took some small bites, a little toast, some bacon, a little egg. I narrowed my eyes as she continued to watch me, maybe the food was poisoned... I looked at the food, then back at her.

She laughed as she realized what I was thinking, and walked over and picked up a piece of toast from the plate, laid a piece of bacon on it and dipped it in the egg and started eating.

"No, it's not poisoned," she said.

"So what gives?"

"I was just amazed, that's all. Here you are, someone I just met a few hours ago, waiting for me before you started eating."

"Isn't that what you're supposed to do?"

"Yes. It is. I just haven't been exposed to such good manners for a long time. My ex-husband the pig-dog used to grunt when I made food for him. Grunt and eat, so I was a little shocked when you asked me if I would be joining you." She went back into the kitchen and made another plate and came back and set it on the coffee table and started eating with me.

"How old are you?" I asked. Her cheeks turned crimson red at the question but she answered.

"Twenty five. Why?"

"I don't know, you just seem too young to have been married and divorced. Way too young if you ask me."

"It happens to the best of people sometimes..."

"How old was the other girl, the one he ran

off with?"

She took a deep breath. "Eighteen."

I nodded. It was hard for her, I could see it in her eyes. "Sorry to be so blunt, but you gotta forget about that guy and move on. I know, I just met you and all, but you gotta wipe that memory out of your mind and never go back. That guy was a jerk. Was, past tense."

She smiled and asked me. "How old are you?"

My turn for the hot seat. "Twenty eight." I tried to get a bite of toast before she asked another question but was too late.

"Don't you think you're a little young to be telling a girl you just met what she should, or shouldn't think?" She arched her eyebrows with a flash of defiant anger, then giggled again and I laughed with her in relief.

"Whew," I sighed. "I thought you were really going to let me have it."

"I was, but thought better of it. Good manners and all."

"Thanks for letting me borrow your couch, I really appreciate it," I said and then mopped the rest of the food from the plate. I waited for her to finish her meal, and grabbed her plate before she could say a word. "I'll do the dishes." She protested and tried to wrestle the plate from my hand but quickly realized it was a losing proposition, and said she would finish getting ready for work.

When I was finished scrubbing and rinsing the plates and putting them in the strainer to dry she came into the kitchen carrying her purse.

"I have to get going, I have a short shift today, just ten hours so I'll be back at six tonight. Here's an extra key." She put it on the counter. "If you need it."

I wiped my hands on the towel and nodded. "I appreciate all you've done for me. I feel like you saved my life."

She bit her lip softly and I reached out and put my arm around her, pulled her close and kissed her. She didn't resist and melted in my arms and when I let go again her eyes stayed closed for a moment like she was in a dream. The best medicine to make her forget about that other guy was to give her someone else to think about, even if I might never see her again. She'd saved my life and I owed her one. She opened her eyes smiling and then looked at the clock and got serious.

"Don't forget the key!" she shouted as she headed for the door, and just like that she was gone.

My natural instinct was suspicion for all things and everyone, and I still could not figure out how a girl that looked that good would be single, no matter what the circumstances of her previous relationship, but there is one thing that I was absolutely dead sure of, when she kissed me back it was the real deal.

I could hear her jogging down the stairs two at a time, and I cracked the drapes to see the little car pull out of the parking lot and merge onto the busy highway. It was six thirty in the morning and the sun was rising in the east over the mountains, while the smog rolled in from the coast where it had rested for the night.

I made certain the stove was off and cool to the touch and went to the door and looked back at the couch, probably the most comfortable place I'd slept in the past few years. I stared at the key sitting on the counter where she'd left it, and thought about taking it with me, just for a moment thought about walking back over there and picking it up. Just in case I needed it. A port in the storm. And then that moment passed. It was too dangerous. I was too dangerous for a pretty little nurse like Amber Clark to be around until I cleared up this little problem of a missing singer.

I cracked open the drapes again and scanned the area outside, then finally satisfied that it was safe, I opened the door and walked out.

6.

The city bus stop was right outside the little apartment complex and was packed at this hour of the morning. It seemed like everyone who lived within a block of this stop was either going to work or school and I found a place near the shed to wait.

I pulled my hat over my eyes and watched the crowd. There was every sort of character you could imagine, every age and size and color and position in society, from a couple of guys in suits and ties to maids and plumbers and students, old people, babies.

I blended in well and kept my mouth shut. Blacks, Asians, Whites, Chicanos, there was even an American Indian looking guy with a Mohawk. The bus top was a melting pot.

A guy standing nearby smoking a cigarette asked if I had change for a twenty and I just shook my head and kept my eyes straight ahead. Mute.

Busses came and went and the crowd

thinned out, and filled up again. Pretty soon a bus rolled up with the sign on the front that I was waiting for, city center it said, and after the remainder of the crowd got on, I followed and stood in the aisle holding onto a strap while the bus lumbered and rolled down the highway belching smoke out the rear end.

Riding on a city bus was about the best way to get around town without catching anyone's attention. The unwashed masses took the bus, and it was like an underground sort of railroad leading from the slums to the promised land and all points in between.

I knew people were looking for me and I needed to travel in secret, in a crowd. I was heading back to the scene of the crime, the intersection where the star got nabbed and I lost my bike and my memory.

I figured that'd probably be the best place to start. It was Bell and Henshaw, that much I remembered and I stepped off the bus on Bell street two full blocks from the intersection and walked slowly, taking in the scene.

There was a mixture of strip malls and residential neighborhoods and apartments along the four lane street, metered parking on both sides. I kept my head down and my eyes up scanning the entire cityscape in front of me as I walked. It was still early morning, not yet seven thirty and the morning rush was in full swing.

I found a place along a wall with an alcove and parked myself in the shadow and watched the intersection up ahead. Bell and Henshaw.

Two nights ago I'd rolled through here and the next thing I knew I was waking up in a hospital. Someone around here knew what happened. The set-up was planned well in advance, and someone close by was in on it.

I heard a siren in the distance, and it seemed like it was heading this way, winding through the streets nearby, the wailing sound dimming and increasing in volume as it travelled.

The funny thing about being near any city, around this many people crammed into a small area, there's always some sort of trouble, and sirens become a way of life, background noise that you get so used to that you don't even notice it, like birds in the countryside that you don't really hear until someone mentions it and you perk up your ears and say, why yes, those birds are chirping rather loudly, I never even noticed they were here.

It was a police car blasting down Bell street, hell bent on getting somewhere in a hurry. All the cars on the street pulled over into the slow lane and the police car took the center line head on, splitting the difference and blazing towards the intersection which had red lights showing on all sides stopping the traffic so the cop could get through without worrying about getting T-boned by a car coming through.

And then I knew.

That was it.

That's how they got me. The bastards. Modern traffic lights are wired together at an intersection, and when an emergency vehicle needs to get through an intersection all the driver needs to do is hit a button which triggers a strobe light on the top of the vehicle that points at a sensor on the traffic light and all the lights turn red and he just sails on through.

After I went through the light on the bike, someone hit a switch and the light turned red and the car with the star and the escort all had to stop. Once I was out of the way the rest was easy. They knew I was somewhere out front, on a private security convoy like this, the perimeter guy is always out front, and once I was out of the picture they moved in. They couldn't have known who I was, what I was driving, but when I turned around they pegged me, the guy on the motorcycle. It all happened right here.

There was a curve in the road and I slowed the bike, downshifting gears so I wouldn't use the brake and alert anyone that it was me, the guy on the bike that was the perimeter guy turning around. I remembered. I did everything right, all according to the book.

It was right here, I was standing right next to the curve in the road where I turned around and I scanned the buildings around me. Someone could have been watching from a second story window, or hiding in a car parked along the road. This is where I lost it, a block and a half from the intersection.

Across the road was a Chinese restaurant, an apartment building, and an abandoned store that looked like an old department store that suddenly went out of business, windows both boarded up and missing along the front like teeth missing from a smile.

An old oriental man was sweeping the steps of the restaurant, bent over from a long life of work no doubt, meticulously moving the flat broom along the corners of each step, sweeping the dust from the previous night into the flower garden on the side, getting ready for another day of business. At least one business was still going strong while the one next to it looked like a wreck.

Besides the empty store and the restaurant, everything else along that side of the road was either a home or an apartment building.

The goons from the agency who were questioning me in the hospital said that someone had found me in an abandoned building, hours after the incident. That was the building, next to the restaurant, I was sure of it. I decided to take a walk across the street and see what was on the menu.

The good thing about the way I looked, semi light, semi dark, not too tall, not too short, light to medium build, basic features, unobtrusive stance and walk and demeanor, I was the average Joe on the street, or Jose, I looked like most of the people you would see on an average day almost anywhere in any country.

I could fit in, and blend in just about anywhere. When I looked up and down the street, there were about ten other guys who kind of looked just like me, and that was a good thing.

Hat down and eyes forward, I walked half a block up and away from the restaurant, waited for the traffic to ease and shot across the street, blending back into the cars parked on the sides.

He saw me coming from far away, that much I was sure of. He kept sweeping the dust into the garden, but I could see him watching me in the hidden corners of his eyes.

When I got closer to the restaurant he moved off the steps and started sweeping the sidewalk in front, pride in his place in life, his little slice of heaven no doubt.

I stopped in front of the big window and read from the menu. They had all the good stuff, kung pao chicken, fried rice, ...

"Good moring," he said cheerfully in broken English. "You hungwy yes?"

I nodded. It was still early. "What time do you open?" I asked him.

He lit up. "Open now, always open, always open, you go in, go in." And he shuffled me up the stairs and through the door leaving the broom on the doorstep but still sweeping, in a way sweeping me into the dining room and seating me at a table near the side window that looked onto an alleyway and the abandoned store.

I sat on the side facing the doorway and angled my chair so I could see behind me and the rest of the dining room. He put a menu in front of me and hustled to the back of the restaurant towards the kitchen.

I could hear some hushed discussion back

there and kept my ears open wide for trouble. It wasn't long before a younger version of the old man came out of the kitchen wearing a cooks apron. The way he walked reminded of a cat, the way they walk on the pads of their feet, slow and methodical, ready to pounce at a moment's notice.

He didn't look too happy to see me, nothing like the old man, that was for damn sure. He stood next to the table staring at me, like he wasn't sure what he was looking at or what to say, he looked confused and angry at the same time, mostly angry though, simmering under the skin, I could see it. Not one bit of happy happy joy joy thought was in this guy's mind.

"We're closed," he said finally.

I measured him for a moment, and gestured towards the old man who was standing by the kitchen door. "He said you're open."

"I don't like cops."

"I'm not a cop."

"I didn't say you were."

"Then what are you saying?"

"I don't like cops, because cops mean trouble, and I don't like trouble, so I don't like cops."

"I told you before, I'm not a cop."

"I know that."

"This conversation is going nowhere," I said.

"I know you're not a cop, because they're the ones looking for you."

"Oh."

"Yeah, they were here earlier this morning, real early, asking questions, showed me a picture of you, said to call them if I saw you again."

"What do you mean, saw me 'again'?"

He looked around the room and out the windows, then motioned the old man towards the front door and spoke in Chinese to him. The old man shuffled back outside and grabbed his broom again, and they could hear the steady sweeping by the steps.

"You're the one they pulled out of the building two nights ago."

"You saw me?"

"I found you."

"What do you mean found me?"

"You ask a lot of questions, just like the cops."

"Don't you think I have a right to know?"

He studied me for a moment, and then nodded. "Alright. We came home real late that night, like two in the morning, the restaurant was closed. When we got back to the intersection two blocks down was closed, cordoned off, so we had to go around to get here. I was in the kitchen putting away the supplies, cleaning up when I heard a sound in the abandoned building next door. We'd been robbed a few times, and sometimes the guys who did it would camp out right there."

"So you heard a sound. Thought I was a robber."

"Yeah, so I grabbed my bat and a flashlight

and went on a little patrol. I go in there all the time, I call it cleaning up the trash."

"Isn't that kind of dangerous?" I asked.

He grinned. I could see it in his eyes. He didn't like trouble but he liked danger, he knew how to handle it, could probably handle me right now with a karate chop to the head. "Yeah, it is," he said, "very dangerous."

I think he meant for the other guy. "So you found me..."

"Yeah, you were hurt, looked like you'd crashed through the front of the building and went right on through a couple of walls to the back."

My side twinged where the ribs were broke, and my head still remembered some of the throbbing pain.

"Was my bike there?"

"What was left of it."

"What does that mean?"

"It was stripped, wheels, handlebars, engine."

"The frame?"

"Naw, it was all twisted, worthless. Plus it was wrapped around a metal pipe, they probably couldn't get it off the pipe, so they just took everything else."

"Where was I?"

"Right next to the metal pipe, I guess the bike's frame saved you."

"So they stripped the bike and left me to die?"

He grinned again. "Like I said, it's a dangerous neighborhood."

"You're telling me."

"You actually didn't look too bad, I was surprised. I think that motorcycle you were riding took most of the brunt of the damage, you must have just followed along after it as it was crashing through all those walls."

"But I was out cold?"

"Snoring actually."

Like a log that sleeps, I thought. He pulled something out of his pocket and handed it to me. It was a slug from a bullet, a large caliber bullet, from a rifle, flattened on one end and round on the other.

I've seen this type of spent projectile before, and I know how it's caused. This is what you get when you fire a sniper rifle at a bullet proof vest. The kind I was wearing that night.

"Where'd you find this?" I asked him.

"My Grandpa. He likes to sweep, likes to keep the steps and the sidewalk clean. He even goes out into the street and sweeps out there. Cars have to go around him. He found it that morning."

"Right out front?"

"Almost directly in front of our front door. There's a skid mark where a motorcycle tire took an abrupt turn to the side."

"My motorcycle."

He nodded. "The track went right into the store."

It was midnight when we left the mansion in the security convoy with the star, heading towards the city. Midnight in a bad part of town when someone tricked the intersection light, and then shot me off my bike.

"You're Grandpa told me that you're always open, but you said you were closed that night."

He narrowed his eyes. Asking a lot of questions again, like the cops.

"Sorry," I said.

He relaxed a bit. "We worked a function that night, catered a little party in the city, said they wanted the whole restaurant there, paid good money."

"Last question," I said. "And then I'll be on my way."

He sighed and nodded so I continued. "Who paid you to host the party?"

He grinned. "He looked kind of like you."

My eyes narrowed.

"I don't mean he looked exactly like you. He had lighter skin, taller, thinner, but he had the same look in his eyes. Yeah he was ex-military no doubt about it, and I don't mean someone sitting at a desk, if you know what I mean."

I knew what he meant. Someone with a gun in the middle of a war zone. That kind of 'like me'.

I got up to leave. "Thanks for the info."

"There's one other thing," he said.

"What's that?"

"He had this little scar right here." And he pointed to his cheek under his left eye. "It ran down this way almost like a tear from his eye. Like he was crying a scar."

Like he was crying a scar. I'd never heard

it put that way before, but I'd seen something like it, once upon a time. An unusual mark on any face. Put it on an ex-military guy who looked 'kind of like me', and the potential suspect base narrowed quite a bit.

"I owe you one," I said and made my way towards the front door.

"Use the back entrance," he said. "I'll show you the way. Just one thing though."

"What's that?" I asked.

"Don't ever come back." There was no grin this time, and I nodded.

"I don't plan on it. This neighborhood is a little too dangerous for me."

7.

I zigzagged through the back alleyways and to a bus stop three blocks from the restaurant and got on the first one that came through. It wasn't going the direction I wanted to go, but it's always prudent in this type of situation to throw a little misdirection at anyone who might be following. I watched the cars that were on the same path as the bus as we travelled through the streets, noted the type and color of each one, and then when the bus stopped at a covered stop I got off and waited in the shade with my back against a pillar and studied the perimeter.

No hairs were standing up on the back of my neck, no fear tingling the corners of my mind, there was nothing. I didn't feel safe, but I didn't feel like I needed to fight or flee either.

I knew I was down to the last couple of dollars of the Eraser's cash and I needed to pick up some walking around money so to speak. After what I'd found out at the Chinese restaurant it looked like I was in it a little deeper than I had thought at first, if that was even possible.

My old man had another old saying, plan for the worst and hope for the best, and lucky for me I'd done a little planning for something like this. Something where I might need to disappear into the woodwork for a while. I was a security guy for the top one percenters, and I knew that with level of money there was bound to be some dirt and grime on the sidelines, and if I ever saw the wrong thing, or made the wrong move, or let someone in my charge get hurt or killed, then I would be one needing security. It was that simple.

I knew I couldn't go to my bank, just waltz right in and make a withdrawal. They'd be watching. I had an emergency fund for just this scenario, but it would take some effort to get to it. I had my own little safe deposit box at my own little bank, the kind of bank you could get to into on the weekend and the middle of the night if you needed. Griffith Park was located on the outskirts of the city, one thousand acres of hills and trees. Lots of places to hide things.

On December 16, 1896 Colonel Griffith J. Griffith, a newspaper reporter turned mining magnate donated three thousand acres to the city of Los Angeles as a Christmas present. He was a true one percenter who got to the top the old fashioned way, by using inside information on mining operations to turn a dollar into millions, and his stated purpose in gifting the land to the city was to make it a 'happy, cleaner and finer city'. A few years later in 1903 during an alcohol fueled bender at the posh Arcadia Hotel in Santa Monica, the good old Colonel shot his wife in the face as she knelt on the ground pleading for her life.

No one knew until then that the Colonel was a mean ass drunk who didn't take kindly to any back talk. His wife lost an eye, and survived, but the marriage did not. She was granted divorce on the grounds of cruelty of all things, and awarded custody of their only child, Vandell. Griffith spent two years in San Quentin and died a few years later in 1919 of liver disease.

The park that carried his name actually was a happy clean and fine place to visit, most of the time.

Sure, there was the occasional riot, mugging and robbery that happened now and then, but that sort of thing could happen just about anywhere where you put two people in close proximity to each other, human nature being what it is.

It took an hour to get there, but it gave me time to plan. The bullet in my pocket was a tough one, and I tried with all my might to remember what had happened that night, but it was all still a blur. I couldn't remember the last moments of being on the bike, no memory of being shot or knocked off the bike or crashing into the building, nothing, it was all a blank. The Chinese restaurant guy said I didn't look too bad after crashing through all those walls, but my ribs told me different. I'll bet if I could take a look at my flak jacket it would have a big dent in it, right about where my ribs were located.

The bus let me off at Griffith park, it was around five in the afternoon and my stomach was growling. There was a large iron gate with an arch and a giant copper G in the middle of it. The patina on the copper had turned it a greenish gold and I wondered why no one had pried it off and tried to peddle it to a metal recycler.

There was a pack of panhandlers with signs telling you what they needed, money for food, for clothes, one guy was honest and had a sign that said he needed money for beer. There were folks handing out flyers for tourist attractions and rides, and tattoo parlors and everything in between. I took a couple of flyers to have something to read, and walked past them all, panhandlers included without a word. Their pans would have to wait. I was down to my last three dollars and I needed two of those to take the bus back to the city in case my safe deposit box had taken a walk. There was a hotdog stand at the entrance selling dogs for two bucks a piece, which put them out of my league. I decided to try to bargain for one, maybe I could get one for half price.

"How about half a dog for a buck?" I asked.

The guy behind the table looked me up and down then ignored me and kept yelling at the crowd.

"Hey hot dogs heeeahhh, get your hot dogs!"

Like he was at a baseball game working the fans. He was short and stocky and middle aged with some gray showing around the edges of his jet black hair and handle bar mustache. Italian or Chicano, it was hard to tell. Either way he was a hard case.

I tried again, this time with a smile. "What do you say friend, half a dog for a buck?"

He broke away from his busy chatter and looked at me with disdain. He pointed a thick finger at me in warning. "I aint your friend pal, so why don't you move along, you're disrupting my business."

The crowd from the bus had thinned out, and we stood there nearly alone under the arches with the G in the middle. I pointed to the mountains and the long golden rays of the impending sunset.

"The day is short and the crowd is waning." I pointed to his grill which had over a dozen reddish dogs cooked and ready to go. "We wouldn't want them to go to waste now would we?"

He narrowed his eyes and gave me his full attention. I had the feeling that if he took a drink of water at that point in time, steam would jet out of his ears. "Oh don't you worry about that," he hissed. "They never go to waste. I'll feed them to the trash can before I'll feed them to a freeloader like you esse."

So he was a Chicano, or maybe he just talked like one.

"Why so harsh at the end of a nice day?" I asked him. "We're both here on Earth, created by the same God."

I pointed to the cross hanging around his neck on a chain. "Don't forget to be compassionate to the poor. I'm not asking for a handout my friend. Just half off the retail price."

He shook his head slowly from side to side and his eyes narrowed. "You see all these deadbeats around here? Their job is begging for money, that's their job, their occupation. They get up in the morning and put their hand out as their career. Grown men and women with the God given strength to go out in the world and work for a living and they choose to live like beggars in the street. Bums. I could spit on them but I wouldn't want to waste the spit. You hear where I'm coming from esse? They all know better than to come around here begging food from ME, I'll make them howl for their stinking lives with a fork in their hand and their face on the grill."

He grinned then, a mean semi-vicious toothy grin framed by the bushy moustache, I could see he was short one tooth up front that probably went missing in a fist fight, and I had the feeling that the scene he just described with the fork in the hand and the face on the grill had actually happened at some point in the past. A few of the panhandlers on the side were watching the verbal exchange with interest and I glanced over there to see if any of them had grill burn scars on their faces.

"Again, I'm not asking for a handout, just half off. All I have is a single dollar. Besides, we're on the same team."

He narrowed his eyes again. "The same team? What the hell are you talking about?"

I pointed to my hat that I'd bought in the thrift store, and then to his.

He laughed. "So you're a Dodgers fan, huh?"

I nodded. "My blood runs Dodger blue."

"Anyone can buy a cap."

"It was Grandpa's." Which could have been true, hell I bought it in a thrift store, it could've been grandpa Sandy Koufax's for all I knew.

He pointed at me while managing a slight grin, and waggled his finger. "Alright, so you want to play with me eh? I'll tell you what. Let's have a little fun. You answer two trivia questions and I'll give you a whole dog for a buck, you can't answer them, you give me the dollar and high tail it the hell out of here. Deal?"

I shook my head. "You could give me some bizarre off-the-wall trivia question that no one knows the answer but you."

"These are easy. If you really are a true Dodger's fan like you claim to be, you'll know the answers. If not, you'll be exposed as a liar. A dirty filthy liar." He threw that last line in there just to call me out.

"Why two questions?"

"In case you get lucky on the first one."

"Alright," I said. "Let's play."

He clapped his hands together and pointed to the table. "Dollar first, on the table, next to the fork."

Next to the fork so he could stab me in the back of the hand if I lost and tried to make off with the bill.

"Alright, alright," I said and I carefully unfolded a dollar bill and placed it on the table and he put the fork on top of it.

"So it doesn't blow away in the wind," he grinned.

I waited patiently for the first question as my stomach grumbled. A couple of the panhandlers inched closer to hear the verbal exchange, staying just out of fork range.

"First question," he began. "When the Dodgers moved to Los Angeles from Brooklyn, what day was their first game, who was their opponent, and what was the score?"

"That's three questions."

"It's a combo. If you don't know the answer, just admit it and walk on. It's the easiest question in the book pal, like you're up to bat and I'm throwing softballs to you underhanded. Baby questions."

I smiled. It was time to put a fork in this guy for a change. I'd had enough playing around, I was hungry.

"The first game on the West coast was on April 15, 1958 in San Francisco, the Dodgers got their asses kicked by the Giants eight to nothing."

He squinted at me and his mouth quivered at the corners, I could he tell didn't like to lose.

And then his eyes glinted, and narrowed. He had something up his sleeve. The first question was a set-up.

"Who was the losing pitcher for the Dodgers, and who made the last out?"

I shook my head in pain, and gritted my teeth and that made him grin wider, he thought he had me, thought he would be sending me off and pocketing my dollar bill, but I knew the answer. Two of the most famous pitchers ever in Major League baseball pitched on that day. Don Drysdale for the Dodgers, and the great Ruben Gomez for the Giants. I knew this because my Dad was a diehard Dodger's fan, and his younger brother, my uncle Manny was a diehard Giant's fan. How that scenario ever came to be no one really knew, but the verbal brawls were intense, and sometimes the verbal brawls turned into fistfights. Family reunions during baseball season were brutal. My Grandpa told me that all brothers needed something to fight over, and the Dodgers Giants rivalry was as good enough a reason as any.

Whenever the arguing got especially heated, uncle Manny would bring up the Rueben Gomez story. When Reuben's fastball slowed down and he wasn't good enough for the Majors anymore, the Giants let him go and he went down south and pitched in the Mexican League. One day he was approached by a young boy desperate for money and selling lottery tickets. Normally Rueben stayed away from any type of gambling but wanted to help the young man out so he bought a ticket which turned out to be the winning ticket worth thirty five thousand dollars. He tried to share the money with the boy's family but they were ashamed and refused, so Rueben set up a trust account for the young man to be given to him when he turned eighteen.

Many years later Rueben was dying of cancer and was in a hospital about to have surgery when a young doctor from Mexico asked to attend the operation. When Rueben asked him why he wanted to attend, the young doctor told him that he was the young boy who sold him the lottery ticket, and the trust fund helped him through medical school.

"Don Drysdale," I said, "was the Dodgers losing pitcher, and Rueben Gomez was the pitcher who made the last out for the Giants."

And his grin disappeared.

He shook his head slowly. "No esse, who made the last out for the Dodgers, you know, who was our guy that was put out."

"You bastard." I whispered. He saw the look in my eyes and stepped back a few inches smiling the whole time and lifted his shirt on the side to show the handle of a gun. Everyone was packing in this town. This guy would shoot me over a dollar bet on some stupid Dodger baseball trivia. This was a tough town. He was close enough that I could lunge across the table and crush his larynx before he could pull the trigger, or I could pull my own gun and shoot him in the hand before he could get me. A guy has to know his options. My stomach lining was tearing itself apart. I didn't know who made the last damn out for the Giants, I couldn't think straight. I was starving. Uncle Manny would know the answer though. And I thought back to one gut wrenching argument in the back yard during a barbecue. That first game ended with a high fastball thrown by Rueben and the last batter struck out swinging. The batter had a funny nick name, and it was his last year in the majors.

The hot dog bully looked happy. "Give up? Can't answer a little trivia question can you?"

I shook my head and smiled. That was it, little. The word triggered a memory and I could see in my mind's eye my Dad and Uncle face to face at the backyard barbecue yelling at each other over the last play of that game. It was a funny little nickname. "Pee Wee Reese struck out swinging. Final play of the game."

He yelled in pain and threw his fists in the air, punching at the sky, and then resigned to his fate, his face relaxed and he smiled slightly, beaten at last.

"My man Pee Wee Reese," he said while catching his breath and sighing. "Stood up for Jackie Robinson all those years when the going was tough in Brooklyn. A lot of folks were against having a black player in the major leagues, but Pee Wee was there to cover his back. I guess you really are a Dodger fan."

And then he reached over with his tongs, pulled the most perfect foot-long dog off the grill, placed it carefully in a bun like he was putting a baby into a crib, and handed it to me.

I looked over at the pile of bums nearby who were beaming with happiness, I had beaten their arch rival, their nemesis who tortured them all day with the sights and smells of a hotdog stand. I picked out the grimiest of the bunch, a white haired old salt with tattered clothes and soiled hat, and called out to him. "What do you like on your dog, mustard or ketchup?"

The old man smiled a toothless smile and answered gently. "A little of both would be most welcome sir."

So I loaded the hotdog with mustard and ketchup and a little relish for good measure, tore it half and handed it to my newest fan. He bowed his head to me in silent thanks, growled at the hot dog man and shuffled off to the side with his treasure.

"You play a good game," said the vendor. "I would have bet this hot dog stand and everything in it that you couldn't answer those questions.

"Why do you have to be so damn mean to these guys. They seem harmless."

"Those guys? They'd stab me in the back if I let my guard down. In fact one of them did stab me in the back a few years ago, and that's why I carry this piece. Don't worry esse, I have a permit, conceal carry, but I don't conceal it, they all know it's right here in plain sight if needed. I show it to them every day, just to remind them and to let any of the new bums that show up that I'm not one to be messed with."

8.

The hot dog went down easy and filled the empty hole in the pit of my stomach, and when I was finished I walked into the park for about a quarter of a mile, and then headed up a hill near the fire road and picnic area. It was about a hundred feet high, with a nice round umbrella tree on top.

I sat down under the large tree and put my back against the rough bark. It was shady and cool and I scanned the horizon and made a note of all the activity, the people, dogs, birds, clouds, fence lines, vantage points, escape routes, branches and rocks that could be used as weapons in a pinch. Satisfied with the result, I pulled my cap down and read the pamphlets while keeping one eye on the perimeter.

The picnic area below had ten tables arranged neatly in two rows on a grassy lawn next to the fire road. There were shade trees and barbecue stands, and faucets for water, and it had a nice wide view of the surrounding mountains and foothills. I could see that the trash cans were full and it must have been busy with a lot of people earlier in the day, but now there was just one young couple and it looked like they were getting ready to leave. He was folding the table cloth while she packed the leftover food into their carry bag.

I couldn't tell if they were newlyweds, or newly engaged, or just out on a date, but he was doing all the right things.

I studied his actions. He was attentive and polite to her, helping her with the leftovers, wiping down the table and tossing a small bag in the trash can and raising his hands at the basket. She applauded his athletic skill. Whatever he was doing to make her happy it was working.

I told myself that if I ever had a chance to have a good woman to impress, I'd be just like that guy.

They were happy and laughing, and she poked him in the stomach with her index finger and he pulled her close and kissed her for a long time.

They were oblivious to the world around them, and for that moment in time, the only world that mattered was each other.

Let them have their fun, I thought, pretty soon it would be dark and they'd be heading down the hill and out of the park and I can get to work.

I went back to reading the pamphlets. There were a lot of fun things to do around here. The park wagon rides were ten dollars apiece and went out into the hills every hour till dark. Sodas were half off with the attached coupon, and burgers were made to order at Ye Olde Snack Shoppe. A Jazz band called The Cufflinks was playing at the Greek Theatre on Friday night under the stars. There was a two for one special at the Tattoo Parlor on Main Street, and half an hour at the gun range was a hundred and twenty five bucks plus ammo.

The Jazz band under the stars sounded like a great event to go to. I imagined a saxophone and trumpets and a thick rambling bass line taking you to another world full of wondrous sound. I made a note to check it out if and when I got out of the trouble I was in. I'd come back up here and sit in the audience and take a trip to the stars riding on a sax.

It's a strange feeling that you get when you start to feel that something is wrong. Something bad is about to happen. A creeping feeling that starts on the back of your neck and makes its way to the top of your head and then down and into your chest and your heart. Your breathing slows and your eyes narrow to a focus and your ears turn up their volume and even your skin tunes in to the vibrations of the world like a living breathing radar system while you strain with every core sense that you have to identify the source of the impending doom. It's not really a sixth sense, it was more like the combination of all the senses in hyper drive, there could be something that you ever so slightly see or smell or hear, something, or a couple of something's on the edge of your peripheral senses trigger your entire being to go on alert, a survival mechanism from the caveman days when things that wanted to eat you would try to sneak up on your when you were sleeping.

An ancient warning.

The Indians used to say that the body did not have five separate senses, they were all one and the same with the world around us, and if you could relax your mind and let the force of nature blend with your spirit, then you would be invincible.

With the tree at my back I scanned the entire scene in front of me. There were hikers on the far ridge, joggers on the fire road far below, condors circling in the sky high above, riding the rising heat waves, their wings rigid and stiff while their feathers on the edges like fingers ruffled with the changing currents. There were squirrels everywhere it seemed, blending in perfectly with their semi brown fur and then becoming visible as they quick scurried here and there, short bursts of speed, rapid fire up and down trees and across roads, then back again. Black crows by the dozens screeching and cawing that blood curdling sound.

The picnic lovers were taking their sweet time wrapping up their luggage, and then on the edge of the horizon where the fire road went over the hill two figures appeared, a man and a boy it seemed at first, and then as they made their way down the road I could see it was a big man and a small man, both had long pants and t-shirts and running shoes, one with a black beanie and the other with a wide rimmed brown fedora, a cowboy type hat, walking close together and talking while scanning the road ahead of them.

The big guy lumbered as he walked, heavy feet and hands, with a thick neck that cradled a Neanderthal head, shaved hair with a pony tail at the back, with a tattoo on his neck that went all the way around it like a collar, a dog collar. The small man with the beanie, light and wiry, also with a shaved head but no pony tail or tattoo on his neck carried a soccer ball cradled in his heavily tattooed arm, and when they saw the couple at the picnic table they slowed their pace and the short one dropped the soccer ball on the ground and began to dribble it as he walked, passing it to the big guy who passed it back, and they laughed as they played the passing game while getting closer to the couple. The little guy even threw in a limp to his walk, dipping on his left side as he made his way down the dirt road.

Their demeanor had changed from quiet conspiratorial talking to happy feet and chatty faces. It was a small change, so subtle that no one would have noticed. No one should have noticed. But I noticed, I saw the change, they were lying bastards, trying to pretend they were something other than what they really were. Crooks on a mission. Their body language tipped them off, whatever mischievous deed they were planning was in full play now.

The picnic table was out in the open and when they passed by they waved and said hello to the couple who politely waved back. The boyfriend was necessarily cautious and waved with a frown. The soccer players passed by and continued down the road and around the corner while joking and passing the soccer ball. The picnic table was too out in the open, too visible. They would lie in wait around the corner and ambush the couple, of that I was certain.

I got a slow sinking feeling in the pit of my stomach as I realized there was no easy way out of this.

The sun was an orange orb sinking into the hazy west as I made up my mind on how I was going to handle the situation. There were a few different ways to play this hand, I could escort the couple out by walking behind them as though I was just another tourist, going the same direction as they were. I could go down and warn the couple to go out a different way, both of which would diffuse the situation peacefully. But that left the problem of the two criminals planning with bad intent to do harm, rob or worse. If not this couple it would be someone else, maybe even me who would get ambushed and beaten later on in the evening.

Time to take out the trash.

I made my way over the ridge behind me, crouching low so the couple wouldn't see me exit the area. The other side of the rise was covered in dry brush and it hid me as I headed towards the curve in the road below. I could see that the road was empty even though by now the tattooed travelers should be right there in plain sight. I was careful not to make a sound, stepping lightly and avoiding the dry branches littering my path, and then I spotted them through a bush, crouching next to a jumble of boulders next to the road with their backs to me. The short thin crook held a gun loosely in his hand while the big guy had a knife. The barrel of the gun was dull black and square, a Glock, probably a .45 with a maximum of thirteen bullets in the magazine. I'd have to take him out first, and then the big guy with the knife.

When I was in basic training in the Army, our self-defense instructor always said that if you're close enough for a karate chop, you're too close, and every time I got into this sort of situation I thought of those words. No way I was gonna get close enough to a karate chop from the big tattooed guy with the knife.

I pulled my gun, checked the chamber and saw the bullet, and headed forward. There was a line of shrubs in front of me and I slid forward quickly while using them as a shield. Close enough now to hear them talking in low hushed tones. The big guy with a guttural mumble while the little guy had an inner city jittery slang.

"Whatchu tink huh Eddie?," said the big guy. "Dey gonna hava lota money, prolly got a new car too."

"Yeah," said the little guy. "I'm gonna off

that boyfriend of hers and ride around in that brand new car with her sitting right next to me."

"Eh, whata bout me?"

"You can ride in the back Honcho, plenty of room to stretch out."

"Maybe she wantsa ride inna back with me eh? Heh heh."

"Don't get stupid, she's riding up front with me."

Honcho boiled with anger. "Don't call me stupid, I warned you Eddie!"

"Alright, alright don't get crazy then. I've got a gun and you've got a knife, what are you gonna do?"

"I'll cut you in half if you call me stupid again." He gripped the knife tight, his knuckles turning white, while Eddie turned the gun and pointed it at the big guys stomach.

"You ever seen a guy die from a gut shot Honcho? Sometimes takes weeks, months even, but they die in the end, they always die." It was a Mexican standoff in a way with the two of them face to face behind the boulder, and then far off in the distance around the bend of the road you could hear the sweet sound of a girl giggling with laughter.

"Here they come," hissed Eddie. "Get ready." And they crouched lower behind the boulder, peering over the edge of it, thoughts of battling each other gone for now as their prey approached.

I was close enough now to spit on them, and I raised my gun to shoulder height and whispered. "Drop the gun or die." They both quickly looked back, eyes wild with fear at the barrel of my gun. The little guys eyes were dilated like pin pricks in the deep hollowed out sockets of his face, a meth head, and he was quick with his response.

"You might get one of us, but not both esse, drop *your* gun or die. Spread out a bit Honcho, make it harder for this punk to hit us both."

While the big guy shuffled to the side Eddie slowly brought his gun around using Honcho's movement as a distraction, and then tried to swing it quick and up towards me. I fired a shot hitting him square in the wrist and his gun clattered to the ground, the silencer on my pistol worked just fine and the only sound was a dull pop from the barrel.

Honcho lunged at me with the knife, too close and fast for me to get off a shot and I ducked under the blade that whistled over my head and caught Honcho flush in the jaw with my right elbow. He flopped on the dirt out cold while Eddie lunged at me from the other side trying to grab at my gun with his good hand. I jabbed him in the ear with my left fist and then with the gun barrel in my right hand broke his jaw in half with a straight right cross, and believe me you can feel and hear the bone break.

He fell face down in the dirt next to Honcho, who was trying to get up, his massive hands scrabbling at the dirt and shaking his head. I could have soccer kicked his head into oblivion but that kind of action can backfire, I could twist my ankle or sprain my big toe, plus it was unnecessary.

On the side of a human's neck run two large ligaments and in between those ligaments is a carotid vessel that brings oxygen filled blood to the brain. There's a pressure point there called the LI-18 that's utilized in acupuncture and fighting. A needle will relieve pressure on the intestine and a karate chop will knock a person unconscious in a split second. I reached down and put my thumb hard into the LI-18 pressure point on his neck and Honcho was out cold again, breathing hard.

"Stay down," I whispered. The flurry of action had taken less than fifteen seconds and I could hear the young couple walking past on the other side of the boulder, oblivious to what had taken place, lost in their own little world together, their shoes scuffling on the dirt road, she giggled and he teased her till they were well out of earshot, their voices fading away down the dirt road.

I picked up Eddie's gun and Honcho's knife and searched them for more weapons. Both had knives strapped to their ankles, and Eddie had a pair of brass knuckles in his pocket along with a metal pipe and a bag with grains of salt, or meth, a few one dollar bills waded up and bits of change. Eddie didn't know that drugs were bad for your health. Honcho was penniless, his pockets full of crumbs and old empty food wrappers. They both stank to high hell and probably hadn't taken a bath in years.

These guys were bad news, and needed to

be locked up and out of the free world. Unfortunately I didn't have time to help them into a paddy wagon. I was in a hurry and needed to get my stash and get the heck out of here. I had no rope to tie them up, and no matter what knock out technique I used on them, they'd eventually wake up and stagger out of here and cause some sort of mayhem in the future.

I slapped Eddies face back and forth till his eyes fluttered and I held the barrel of the gun at the bridge of his nose till he woke up and saw the trouble he was in.

"You see this hombre?" I whispered and he nodded ever so slightly, his eyeballs wide with fear, fluttering in their sockets, jaw throbbing in pain.

"I'll be watching you, and your buddy Honcho over here, wherever you go for the rest of eternity. I'll be in the shadows, waiting for you to mess up again and then I'll put a bullet right between your eyes. You got that? For the rest of time hombre, I'm watching you. Understand?" He nodded and I pushed my thumb into the side of his neck and he went limp. I did the same thing to Honcho but it took a little while longer to get the point across to him. When he came to and saw the barrel of the gun pointing between his eyes he tried to get up and I had to put my knee on his chin till he quieted down, and when I had his full attention I warned him, and he listened and then he went to sleep again with a thumb in his neck.

I had about five minutes till they would come out of their knock out daze and try to walk out of here. Someone would probably see them stumbling around, and call for an ambulance and the police, and then they'd be all over this place.

I jogged to the top of the hill, found a medium sized rock in the middle of a clump of sage brush, rolled it over and dug a small hole, put the knives and Eddies gun into it, filled it with dirt and rolled the rock back in place. A hundred years from now someone might find the weapons and wonder how they got there.

From my vantage point I listened hard, chickadees clicked in every direction and the sound of an odd crow here and there filtered in the breeze. On the hill opposite the dirt road was a large mesquite tree, it's trunk twisted from a storm long ago, twisted into a sort of S shape. S for stash, my stash. My stash of weapons and money.

Dusk was settling in when I got to the S tree. I stood with the back of my heel against the trunk and counted twenty five paces straight north and started digging with my hands. My fingernails scrabbled onto the metal case, grabbed the handle on top and lifted it out of its hole. It was an Army photography equipment case I found at a thrift store, it's amazing what you can find at those places, two cubic feet, waterproof and built for combat action, like being thrown out of planes and run over by tanks on the battlefield.

The latches opened without a hitch and I

could smell the oiled metal of my pistols wrapped in towels. There were four of everything, four Glock thirty fives, four cans of mace, four boot knives, four stun grenades, four hundred rounds of ammo, four mobile phones, four night scopes, and four thousand dollars in assorted small bills. I took half of everything, sealed the case, put it back in the hole and covered it with dirt again, safe keeping in case I needed it again. Then I went back to the mesquite tree, broke off a low hanging branch and carefully swept the area of footsteps, scattered some little rocks across the whole area and headed back down the hill.

It was dark now, not pitch black but the world around me barely visible, the other side of twilight and just the way I liked it, my time of the day. I sprinted down the dirt road, past the big boulder with the crooks laid out on the other side and kept going till I was at the observatory. The place was bustling, star gazers lining up at the entrance for a chance to look through the telescopes, scout troops, families, couples. I spotted a taxi dropping off a couple of Japanese tourists and I jumped in the back.

9.

"How's your eye?"

"It's fine."

"It looks like shit, you should put some ice on it. They say ice is the best medicine for an injury. It takes down the swelling and lets the tissues heal themselves."

"I said it's fine, now mind your own damn business." Jerry Smith AKA 'also known as' the Eraser put down the pen he was writing with and rubbed his forehead near his eye socket that was causing his partner so much concern. He'd been popping aspirin for the past few hours and the throbbing headache near his temple was still there. His partner AKA the Bulldog wouldn't let up.

"If I'd been minding mine as well as your business back at the hospital," said the Bulldog. "We wouldn't be in here writing reports, we'd be outside. You let Badger knock you upside the head and get away. I thought you were smarter than that." He shook his head. "I was wrong."

The Eraser's eyes glazed over while muttering something in another language, then turned to the Bulldog and measured the distance to the tip of the offending chin. He'd have to lunge three feet over the table to connect with a knockout punch. He figured he could get some extra speed and leverage by pushing off the table with his left hand and kicking the chair away with his right foot. It was still a little too far though, it gave the Dog way too much time to block the punch.

"If you'd been watching the door like YOU were supposed to, he never would have skipped, and now we look like a couple of punk rookies who can't even keep watch over a half dead and drugged guy on a gurney in the middle of a crowded hospital."

"One thing I can't understand is how he got out of there so quickly. I was in the bathroom for three minutes tops. Three minutes Jerry. I come out, the nurse tells me that she saw you head out the ward entrance and that was that. I check on the patient, he looks like he's sleeping peacefully, then I notice a little blood near his forehead and I get down and look closer and it's you. I almost jumped outta my shoes. Scared the crap outa me like a horror movie seeing you there."

"Yeah? Imagine how I felt coming out of that drug induced coma that son of a bitch put me in. I thought I'd died and couldn't wake up. I was a zombie for two days. Some kind of horse tranquilizer in that drip."

"The kids pretty crafty though, you gotta admit it. But I hear we got a lot of assets looking for him . He won't stay lost for very long."

Eraser shook his head and looked square at his partner. "They sure better find him before I do. When I get my hands on him, I'm gonna squeeze the life out of him."

"How could he knock you out, change into your clothes, put you in the bed with the needle and get out of there in three minutes, that's what I can't understand."

"How do you know it was only three minutes? Do you run a stopwatch when you go to the toilet? Maybe it was four minutes, maybe it was five. Maybe you were in there for ten minutes or more, looking at yourself in the mirror and telling yourself what a handsome bastard you are."

"We've gone over this Jerry. I went through the motions so to speak and timed myself as I remember, and we interviewed the nurse who confirmed it was around three minutes. The kid is good, you have to admit it."

"I'm gonna kill him when I find him."

They were sitting in a ten by ten room in one of the corner offices. Windows looking out onto the city and the adjacent offices, except for one side where the plane glass was replaced with mirrors. It was more like an interrogation room than an office.

The agency was run like a division of the FBI. Housed on the entire third floor of a gleaming building near the center of the city with glassed in offices and reception areas.

The building was brand new steel and reinforced concrete, windows mirror glazed so you see out, but no one could see in, sniper proof, and the third floor location chosen specifically since it was high enough to prevent an outside intrusion, but not too high to quickly escape in the event of fire or attack. It was swept for surveillance bugs twice a day since the information on who they were protecting, the where and when and how they were being protected could wind up in the wrong hands and get someone killed, or worse. A security firm's first order of business was securing itself. Triple background checks were done on all the employees and was continually updated, an entire wing of the firm was devoted to tracking its own employees.

The head of the organization was at one time second in command at the FBI, and he modeled the business after it. He saw a need in the private sector, as well as a lot more money for his pocket, and started ESP, short for Elite Security Protection.

With his inside connections he nailed down a couple of prime accounts both foreign and domestic, and cherry picked some of the best and brightest of the agencies, the Secret Service, FBI, CIA, NSA and all the armed services were scoured for workers.

Highly trained by the U.S. government and now highly paid for their services with ESP, the turnover ratio was just about nil. When the money people came to the country they looked for ESP to provide the extra layer of security, and for a guy with a lot of money, money was no object to stay alive. There was no advertising.

ESP employed the best spies, intelligence and muscle in the world. When the Pope came to New York and provided one of the greatest security challenges of the decade, the U.S. government paid ESP to provide an added circle of surveillance and protection. They neutralized two hit squads that the public never even found out about. Things didn't go wrong when ESP was involved. Their reputation was built on guaranteed protection, so when the star was nabbed and their guy on the perimeter disappeared, the only thing you could guarantee was that heads would roll.

"Here he comes," said the Bulldog, as he watched through the glass pane window towards the center of the building. A silver haired man walked through the reception areas. Dressed in a black suit and tie, tall and smooth and moving like a cat, alert measured and slow, with two tough looking bodyguards on either side, he nodded at the people working at their desks as he made his way towards the interrogation room. It didn't look like he'd ever smiled in his life.

The larger of the bodyguards opened the door and entered first, there was a good reason for this, since if someone were to start shooting, the bigger guy would offer more blocking for the bullets, standard bodyguard procedure. The head of ESP, at this point in time, didn't trust anyone. The burly bodyguard motioned with his hand and Bulldog and Eraser pulled out their service pistols and slid them across the table. The second bodyguard entered next and brought a small wand out of his pocket and motioned for the two prisoners to stand up. He waved the portable metal detector up and down their sides and put it away without a word. This wasn't a gun free zone by any means. In fact everyone on this floor was packing a weapon, every single employee of the agency was fully trained in self-defense and firearms. The interrogation room however, was a gun-free zone when the boss was in it.

They all sat down at the large square table, the Eraser and Bulldog on one side flanked by the two bodyguards, the silver haired Mason facing them.

Mason wasted no time. "You really screwed up this time Jerry."

"I know, we've been going over the..."

"I didn't ask you to speak." He interlocked his fingers and tapped his forefingers together as he looked at them. "The Sultan of Brunei cancelled the service we had scheduled for next month on their trip to the States, their head of security said they would get back to us for rescheduling sometime in the future. Three days of perimeter security, half a million dollars." His eyes never left the two on the other side of the table.

"The house of Saud has rescheduled their trip to Los Angeles, five days, three quarters of a million dollars in security. Goldman Sachs asked me to reschedule the security arrangement for the Chicago conference. One day perimeter, two hundred and fifty thousand dollars. I'm telling you the financial details so that you both understand the gravity of the situation in which you've placed us. In a single day we have lost one and one half million dollars of contracts. By tomorrow we could be out of business. People don't pay to get killed or kidnapped, they pay SO THEY DON'T GET KILLED OR KIDNAPPED!" He slammed his hand on the table and everyone on the third floor looked over at the glass walled office, then quickly went back to work. "They didn't explicitly say it but we have been removed from their A-list for now, until we fix the situation."

He smoothed his silver hair and sat back in his chair. "Jerry, you set up security for this operation."

"Yes."

"You put one of our best assets on the perimeter."

"Yes. Badger was one of the best we had."

The word 'had' lingered in the air. Past tense. History.

Mason nodded. "We lost four of our bodyguards, and our perimeter guy survived. It's supposed to be the other way around, if there's a problem, it doesn't get past the perimeter. So you were interrogating him to see if he was part of the opposing operation, and he escaped. You had him drugged and incapacitated and he escaped. He assaulted you and escaped and is now somewhere on the loose and at this point in time we have no idea where he is. Correct?"

Jerry nodded. It was pathetic. "I don't think he had anything to do with it, there's no way he would pretend to crash his motorcycle into that building. He was too busted up for real. There was no fake to it, I'm telling you. I don't think he's involved."

"I don't care what you think. I need to know. If you weren't aware of it by now, I don't take chances. Our company doesn't take chances. Our clients don't pay us huge sums of money to take chances. This isn't a casino where you roll the dice and hope for the best Jerry. I need to know without a single doubt that Badger did not have any connection to the other side. Simple as that. I'm not going to take a chance with my hundred million dollar business on what you think."

He unfolded his hands and pointed across the table. "Are those your reports?"

They both nodded and slid them across the table. Mason scanned them and shook his head.

"Unbelievable. It was a simple job, escort the babe to a club and back. She's not even that famous. But, what I've learned over the years is that a small job can up and bite you just as easy as the big jobs."

He brooded, tapping his fingers on the desk as he thought.

"All right, here's the deal. We have all our assets looking for the girl. If we can't find her no one can. And if we can't find her soon, we might as well just close up shop forever. Your job..." and he pointed at them with an angry finger, "... is to find Badger. I don't care what you have to do to get it done. Break down doors, break bones, break faces, break every damn law on the books for all I care, just find that guy. Understood?"

10.

I wanted to get a good look at the competition so to speak. See what I was up against with the agency or whoever else they had on my tail. I needed to find out what type of assets were lined up against me, if any, and there was a quick test I could use.

Heck, I thought hopefully, maybe they'd forgotten about me, given up and moved onto bigger and better things. Maybe they realized that I had nothing to do with the heist, and they were wasting their time looking for me. They had their shot at me and I'd gotten away and now the odds of them getting me back in their clutches was pretty remote. There was one way to find out just how deep their tentacles reached in their quest to find me.

I had the taxi drop me off near a strip mall on the edge of Burbank. The city block was a mix of convenience stores, warehouse type buildings and a one story brick motel, the type where you parked right in front of the room, an air conditioner hanging out of the bottom of a window, and your view was the hood of your car in the parking lot. Convenient, and cheap.

The neon sign at the front said 'Vacancy', and I didn't doubt it for a minute. It seemed a little dirty around the edges, a little seedy and worn, in need of a coat of paint or at the very least a week long rainstorm. The kind of place where you could pay cash for the room, no ID necessary and no questions asked, a place for one night stands and drug deals and fugitives hiding from the law or their exes.

I kept to the shadows as I walked to the office and pulled my cap down over my eyes. This is the kind of place where you wouldn't normally find cameras filming the patrons or they'd lose all their business, but you never could tell these days.

The clerk sitting behind the desk was smoking a long cigarette and squinted at me as I came in the door. There was very large ashtray on the table next to him with a hundred butts in a pile of gray ashes.

He was thin and pale and his skin sucked in around his face and neck as he took another puff of the stick, and let the smoke slowly filter out of his mouth and nose as he watched me.

Dressed in a white tee-shirt and stubbly tinted reddish hair with the smoke streaming up and around his face, he looked like a living breathing cigarette. I wanted to reach over and grab him by his skinny neck, turn him upside down, and put *him* out in the ashtray.

It seemed that his puffing on a cigarette was his method of greeting the customer, so I initiated the conversation. "I need a room for the night. Nothing fancy, single bed will do just fine."

He must have noticed my disdain for his lack of customer service and there was a flicker in his eye. "All we have left is the Presidential Suite."

Wise guy. I didn't see an inkling of a smile on his face or in his eyes and I could tell that he was actually trying to screw with me. I had a choice to make here. These were the kind of people that you generally tried to avoid. A chain smoking crackhead with a death wish. I'm sure he could tell that I was the kind of guy who packed a weapon or two, but he probably had a sawed off shotgun sitting on his lap under the table aimed at my mid-section. I definitely would in this neighborhood, so I didn't argue with him.

"How much?"

"Too fitty."

My face remained emotionless and he took another drag on the cigarette while watching me for a reaction. Too fitty, ghetto slang for two hundred and fifty dollars. A skinny white chain smoking crackhead speaking ghetto and trying to work me over like a patsy.

I shook my head no. "I'll give you one fitty. I only need the room for an hour. Take it or leave it."

He almost smiled at that and seemed to look around me to see if I had a girl with me.

He seemed ready to keep the bargaining going, but looked closely at my eyes and thought twice, then ground the butt of the cigarette into the ashtray and let the smoke evaporate into the air. He was impatient to get me out of there. "Alright. One hour, one fitty. Cash."

I peeled off seven twenty dollar bills and one ten. "Keep the change," I told him.

He shined a little blue pen light on all the bills to make sure they were legit, and folded them into a tight wad. Somehow I had the feeling the money wasn't going into the cash register. He pulled a key off the rack next to his chair and tossed it on the desk. "Room one ten." And then lit another cigarette.

The room itself wasn't too bad, it had a bed, a TV and a bathroom, but it stank like mold and air conditioner fluid and there was a dark stain on the floor near the front door and faded chalk like an outline of a body. No back windows or doors. One way in and one way out, and the guy who made the stain probably went out in a bag. Presidential Suite my eye.

I turned the lights out and opened the drapes a crack and used my night scope to survey the area across the street. I'd already checked it out on my way over here and just wanted a second look from this angle. There were two warehouse buildings side by side and some nooks and crannies where I could hide. It was far enough away that I could get out of there quick if they spotted me. I figured I would have about ten minutes to half an hour after I made the call.

I pulled out one of the cell phones and double checked the address and contact info that was stored on it to make sure it was empty, and then dialed up my ex brother in law Danny Willett. A real piece of garbage, he started beating up my sister about a year after they were married, until I found out about it and broke both his hands with a midnight tap dance while wearing steel heeled boots on a concrete floor.

Still, he was family, sort of, and even though to this day he held the broken hands thing against me, I made it a point to call at least once a year to check in and see how he was doing and to make sure he was staying far away from my sister.

The phone on the other end rang twice and a gruff and burly voice answered. "DW."

"Danny boy, it's your favorite ex-brother-in-law."

Silence on the other end for a moment and the sound of a quick startled breath mixed with a muttered damn and a hell, and his phone clattered to the ground.

Like a Pavlov response his hands remembered the pain of the tap dance and he dropped the phone every time.

He came back on the line again, suddenly less gruff, now that he knew who was on the other end.

"Look I haven't called or seen her in five years, we're divorced, it's over, and I've told you and her I'm sorry a thousand times. What more do you want from me?"

"Keep up the good work," I said and hung up.

Half an hour at the most, ten minutes at the least I figured before someone showed up to pay me a visit. I checked my watch and made a mental note. It was half past eight, and I'm guessing fifteen minutes, so eight forty five is when they'll get here.

I decided to up the ante and make another call, just in case they weren't monitoring the old brother in law. I punched in a ten digit number and it rang five times before a woman's voice answered. She sounded sweet and nice but I knew better.

"Hi this Patti!" A little too perky and bouncy to be real. My ex fiancé, met her in Texas after boot camp when I was in the best shape of my life, flush with cash from the signing bonus and stupid when it came to dirty blondes. Took me for every penny I had when I was over in Baghdad, drained my bank account, wrecked my car, lost my dog, and took out a couple of big credit card loans in my name for good measure.

"It's Badger." And her tone changed instantly, from bouncy to bitchy.

"What do you want? I should just hang up, you bastard. You got your money back, and I did my time in jail. Why do you have to call me every year?"

"Just checking to make sure you're staying out of trouble. Are you?" I could hear the hiss from her breath as she inhaled like a snake on the other end of the line.

"Sure, I'm working down at the soup kitchen for the homeless during the day, and at night I run the bingo games at the old folks home."

Liar, she was probably bilking some poor bastard soldier that very minute. Maybe two or three at once.

"Well that's good to hear," I said. "Tell you what, I'll take a trip down there to see that you're doing just that. Maybe next week."

"Oh I wouldn't if I were you Badger." I could hear the tremble in her voice as it cracked. "I've got a new boyfriend now and he is way tougher than you'll ever be. If you so much as set a foot in this town..."

I hung up and tossed the phone onto the middle of the bed and checked my watch. Two phone calls, three minutes elapsed time and if these guys in the agency were worth their salt they'd have my phone pegged and mapped, and be on their way.

I slid out the door and across the street to the warehouses and found a little cubby hole in one of the little alleyways that led to the next city block and a residential neighborhood. There was a little stairway to a second floor and I could crouch next to the wall and have a good view of the motel with my scope.

The cell phone had a GPS device as they all do nowadays, and all an intelligence agency needed to do was monitor any of the phone numbers that a subject had ever called in the past and when the monitoring computer tagged a call that didn't have a genuine caller ID associated with it, it would trigger an alert with the GPS ID number which could be instantly tracked. And since every phone call on the entire planet was constantly tracked and recorded all they had to do was set up a program and let it run itself.

It took them longer than I had thought to get to the motel. I looked at my watch, twenty minutes I'd been waiting, and I watched with amusement as the scene unfolded.

An old lady came hobbling down the street carrying a shopping bag. She looked about a hundred years old, all bent over and walking as slow as molasses. She turned towards the motel parking lot and made her way towards the building, stopping once in a while to catch her breath and adjust her shawl. Poor thing.

A middle aged man walking by tried to help her and she shooed him off with her cane. When she got close to my Presidential Suite, two black sedans with tinted windows quietly pulled up at opposite ends of the block and parked with their engines running, blocking any escape.

The little old lady paused at my front door and then jumped to the side as a small explosion ripped the door open, she threw off her shawl while tossing a stun grenade through the open doorway.

There was a flash of light in the once darkened room and she pulled a stub nosed gun from the shopping bag and darted into the room while the black sedans burned rubber into the parking lot and nearly crashed into the building while more guys with guns ejected out of the cars and covered the front door and dashed into the room.

After a few short minutes the old lady came out of the door and it turns out she really was a young man with a moustache. Imagine that. I was over half a mile away, but with the night scope I could see the stubble on the old lady's chin. I'd never seen any of these guys before, but the agency was rather large and I'm sure I hadn't seen even one percent of the muscle.

The human cigarette came out of his office to see what all the commotion was about, and was greeted by a couple of the suits. He was busy shrugging his shoulders and shaking his head in full denial of any knowledge of the offending guest and finally put his palms up as if to say "I know nothing."

Back at the room the old lady and the team had concluded their search of the motel room and were gathered outside by their cars. Some of them were scanning the outskirts of the area and I knew that they knew that they'd been set up, that I was watching them and there was nothing they could do about it.

I'd seen all I needed to see and put the scope in my pocket and slid down a pipe next to the building and disappeared down the alley into the night.

11.

They decided to have the news conference in the rotundum of the County building. It was big enough for a large crowd and had good acoustics and had the official County Seal and Motto in the background that would look good on film and make people think that the problem was being taken care of by those in power. The Mayor, the Chief of Police, the head of the protection agency, and C-Dub all walked out together to face the throng of reporters and cameras.

All the major networks were there along with most of their local affiliates. The podium was bustling with microphones fastened together like a giant gray and black mushroom flower in front of them while sound technicians held even more boom mics above the trio to capture every micro-bit of sound. Over a hundred camera lenses were pointing towards them as they walked out, the still cameras clicking with a controlled frenzy, and the police chief though highly trained in crowd control, found himself wiping perspiration off his brow as he looked out at the sea of round glass and serious faces.

The mayor started off. “As you all know, one of the most beloved singers in the entire nation has been abducted on one of our streets, and her bodyguards brutally murdered while trying to protect her. There are a few leads that are being tracked, and we are doing everything we can to get Miss Nightingale back to safety. I have the chief of police, and her manager and fiancé, Mr. Washington here to answer a few questions. So let’s keep this civil and to the point please.”

The place erupted in a shouting and shoving match as every newsman and woman in the building tried to get in the first question. The Mayor pointed at a young woman in the first tier.

“Mayor, when you say you have leads, can you be more specific?”

The mayor nodded to the chief of police who stepped closer to the microphone and cleared his throat.

“From eyewitness accounts and CCTV footage we know that four black SUV’s surrounded Nightingales’ car and the escort vehicle hemming them in and blocking them, five individuals emerged from the attacking vehicles, there was a very brief firefight whereupon the chauffeur and her three bodyguards were instantly killed and

Nightingale was removed from her vehicle and placed in one of the black SUV's. The event took less than thirty seconds to be completed, and the four SUV's all sped off in the same direction, then split up at the next intersection heading in different directions. It was obviously a very well planned out operation."

"Any leads on the cars?" shouted a newsman towards the back.

"There are over fifty thousand black SUV's registered in the city," said the chief. "We have personnel combing through the database."

Another reporter from the back shouted, "If it was a well-planned operation as you say, maybe they just painted the cars black for the job, and now they've been repainted to their original color."

All the eyes in the room turned from the questioner to the chief and his heart skipped a beat. This was exactly the kind of questioning that he was worried about facing. Detailed questioning.

"Look, we have other ways besides color of identifying the vehicles in question, methods that I cannot disclose to you at this time."

"Bullshit," one of the reporters said just loud enough for everyone to hear but not loud enough for him to be identified in the crowd and thrown out on his ear by security.

The chief tried to pinpoint the culprit in the crowd.

"What about a ransom," shouted another pushy newsman from the middle of the crowd. "Have there been any demands?"

The chief nodded his head. "Yes, we have a ransom demand but I can't get into the specifics. We've also had a few crank callers taking responsibility and demanding rewards, but they've all been vetted and we do have a few individuals in custody for making false claims."

"What about ballistics?" Shouted another from the edge. "What type of guns were used?"

Chief shook his head. "I can't disclose that either, but I can tell you they were military caliber."

"Are you saying the kidnappers were military trained?"

"It could be, we're looking into that possibility. Look, these weren't your ordinary bad guys off the streets in East LA. They had this thing timed out to perfection, and we can't rule out the fact that it does resemble a military type operation. We also can't rule out that it was an operation planned in another country."

"Terrorism?" Shouted a few reporters at once.

"No, we think we can pretty much rule that out. As I said before, we have a ransom demand and we believe this is all about money. Next question." In his mind he patted himself on the back, he was getting the hang of it now, putting these jerk reporters in their place. Another shouting match ensued from the throng, and the chief pointed to a well-dressed reporter in the front row. One of Cole's guys.

"Mr. Washington, what about the timing of your record company releasing the album the day after Miss Nightingale was abducted?"

The room grew quiet as C-Dub stepped forward to the microphones and surveyed the crowd. It was about time someone directed a question towards him, and he somewhat relished being in the spotlight.

Might as well get this out of the way. It was a perfect planted question.

"First of all," he began. "My condolences to the families of those brave men who were guarding our Nightingale on that fateful night when she was brutally kidnapped by force. They went to work that night to provide for their families, and they did not return. For that we are truly saddened. You ask about the timing of the album being released the day after that awful event."

The same reporter re-affirmed his questioning. "Yes, some are saying it was publicity stunt gone wrong, or maybe just a publicity stunt with bad intent."

C-Dub. shook his head and surveyed the crowd of reporters with anger in his eyes, and he took his time before responding.

"Well, I have to say there's something sick about the type of people who would insinuate something as devious as that. The album was scheduled to be released on the day that it was in fact released, the wheels were already in motion long before this happened, the album was in the physical stores, the on-line stores were keyed with the digital imprint, and there was no way for us to recall the product even if we wanted to, it was already on the shelves. It's an unfortunate event, but it was out of our control. I tried to stop the release but it was too late."

The same reporter kept up with his line of questioning. "Do you think it would have shot to number one in the world without this 'unfortunate event', as you put it?"

C-Dubs' eyes narrowed. "Are you accusing us of orchestrating this murderous event to sell albums? The hell with you."

"I'm just asking a question Mr. Washington. We're reporters, this is what we do, we ask questions. Do you think that this event contributed to the album's overnight success?"

C-Dub nodded and shrugged his shoulders. "Or course it did. I'd be lying if I said it didn't. Yes, the level of interest in the album increased with the news of her kidnapping. And yes the timing is suspect to people with overly active and suspicious minds like yourself. And yet I also believe that the album would have done very, very well without this terrible tragedy happening, and I do believe it would have eventually gotten to number one on the charts, just not as quickly as it did. However, we're not here to talk about albums, or conspiracy theories. We're here to talk about Gale Nighting and how we are going to bring her back safe. You have my word on that. We have a ransom demand and we are working on putting it together."

The head of the Agency stepped forward to the podium. "We're also here to ask for the public's help in finding one of our agents who went missing after the kidnapping. He held up a glossy eight by ten photo of Badger. "This is one of the bodyguards who was with Gale that night. He survived the attack, and was in a hospital room recovering from his wounds when he stumbled out of bed and somehow made it out of the hospital before anyone noticed that he was missing."

The news reporters looked stunned.

"What?..." was all one of the closest in front could manage.

"Why would he just walk out of the hospital, what was wrong with him?" asked another.

"He has head trauma," answered Mason. "He didn't know who he was or where he was. He has amnesia and has no recollection of the events of the attack and kidnapping. We're asking for your help to find him."

The reporter up front was brutal. "So not only did you lose Nightingale, you lost an agent who was in a hospital bed?"

The entire audience looked as one mass from the questioner to Mason.

The chief felt a twinge in his chest and stepped back up to the podium, not pleased with the question. "Ladies and gentlemen, that concludes our news conference, we need to get back to work finding Gale Nighting. You have the facts of the case and we'll be updating you as events unfold. Thank you."

The place erupted in shouted questions from every angle, and turned into a mob, the cameras and microphones like clubs and spears held aloft by an angry tribe as the Police Chief ushered his entourage out of the rotundum and through an adjacent door that was flanked by heavily armed officers.

12.

I look at my watch and note the time. It's half past midnight in beautiful downtown Brea, and I'm two blocks over from Wilshire Boulevard on the mean outskirts of the swank section of L.A., where everyone in the world wants to be. Hollywood is a few miles to the East, while Beverly Hills is a few miles and a couple of worlds to the north.

Brea in Spanish means tar, La Brea literally means the tar. I'm standing across the street from a club aptly named 'The Pit' in reference to the nearby La Brea Tar Pits, the last resting place of exotic and extinct creatures such as Mastodon Elephants, Saber Tooth Cats, an American Lion, and the Camelops, which is sort of a cross between a Camel and a Llama.

I remembered going there on a field trip with my fifth grade class and going on a tour. It was one of the most fun and informative trips I'd ever been on in school, and I remembered every bit of it, every sight and sound and smell. I loved detailed history and I swam in it, soaked it up like a sponge and wallowed in it like a pig in a swamp.

Just around eleven thousand years ago at the end of the Pleistocene era and the last ice age, the area around present day Los Angeles was teeming with exotic wild life. Mankind had not yet made it this far around the globe, and was still trekking across the Asian continent to the land bridge that stretched across the Bering Strait.

While the glaciers receded at the top of the North American continent, this area was cool and moist, rivers and streams filled with running water, low jungles and grass lands. Along with the big cats and Mastodon's there was even a strange creature called the Harlan's Ground Sloth that grew up to nine feet tall and weighed fifteen hundred pounds.

I couldn't imagine a fifteen hundred pound sloth meandering around on the same ground that was now covered in concrete and buildings, high rises and stores and homes.

For tens of thousands of years asphalt tar seeped and bubbled its way up through cracks in the earth and formed thick sticky pools that were covered with dirt and leaves in the middle of a semi tropical paradise, and when a large hapless animal like the Sloth wandered into the area it became mired in the black glue, hooved feet unable to move and falling over into the pit to die.

Predator animals would come from far and

wide to feed on the dying or dead animal, and also became trapped. Tar pits tended to capture more predators than prey, and the pits are known as predator traps.

A human generation is measured in twenty years, and in the time since Mastodon's and Saber Tooth Tigers and fifteen hundred pound Sloths were running all over this place eleven thousand years in the past, it boiled down to a short five hundred and fifty generations ago that this part of the world was a much different place.

How times have changed.

As I stood in the shadow of the doorway to a dark and shuttered tattoo parlor, I marveled at how far we had come as a species, how far human evolution had advanced and moved forward, since those pre-historic days.

Trash and bottles litter the street, cigarette butts, spit, projectile vomit, gum, graffiti, the works. It was all here. Humanity at its finest. A filthy bum is passed out on the corner, while another searches the trash cans nearby for bottles and cans to trade for booze or worse. Across the street from where I stand, grinding over-amplified metal guitar, grunting lyrics, and pounding drum sounds are oozing from The Pit in the early morning hours. It's a punk rock rap club on the edge of the miracle mile.

This is the place I was heading to with the star on that fateful night. This wonderful place.

There's a doorman at the front of the joint, checking ID's, letting in some people and waving others off. He's short and round with a midsection like a steel trash can, and moves pretty quick for guy his size. Maybe he was a wrestler in the past, I thought, definitely not a boxer, not enough reach with those stubby arms. He looked like the kind of guy you could pepper with jabs, but if you got too close he'd put you in a headlock and squeeze your melon right off your neck.

I've been watching for about half an hour and I can't figure out his method of choosing who goes in or who gets waved off. The ones who do get the approval get a metal detector wand before they get past the bouncer and into the club. He seems to be enjoying himself, the big man at the front of a music hell candy store.

A pack of about a half dozen punkers, shaved heads, metal spikes and leather jackets get waved in, while a couple of stoned surfer types in laid back valley clothes get waved off and practically chased down the street. Then a couple of nearly identical punkers as the ones who got let in, get chased away, while some normal looking patrons get in. It's a pretty popular spot I had to admit, but now with the time winding down and getting close to one o'clock in the morning the line had thinned out to no-one. The bouncer looked agitated, since there wasn't anyone left for him to judge.

I decided to find out if I made the grade and wandered across the street towards the entrance. He saw me coming from far away, and I could see his eyes narrow and a faint little satisfied glint in the corner of his mouth. Another victim, he was thinking.

I smiled and nodded, then pulled out my wallet and showed him my driver's license, the one that said Conrad Pennington III. He checked it front and back, shined a blue light on it to see if it was counterfeit and handed it back.

"Conrad Pennington the third huh, what the hell kind of name is that?"

"I don't know, a regular name I guess."

"You from England?"

"East L.A."

"Bullshit."

"Whittier memorial hospital."

"Sure, the uppity part of East L.A. Doesn't count, doesn't count around here pal."

"You gonna let me in or we gonna stand out here and talk about old times all night?"

"Why should I let you in, we got high standards around here."

Half a block away, a drunk on the street corner was busy hurling in the bushes.

"Yeah, I can tell," I said.

Maybe it was the sarcastic remark that did the trick. He squinted at me and shook his head. "Naw, you aint getting in pal. Ever."

"Why not? Give me a valid reason and I walk away."

"Simple, we aint allowing anyone named Pennington in tonight. Too much of a wuss name."

I measured the distance to his neck, a crisp backhand would do nice right about now.

"I'll tell you what" I reached into my wallet and pulled out five twenty dollar bills, fanned them like a turkey tail, and held them out to him. "I'll give you a hundred bucks to get in."

His face changed color, that really did the trick. "You'll pay a hundred bucks to get in here?"

I nodded. "It's all yours. Just step aside."

" Hand it over so I can count it."

He counted the bills out slowly, then shined the blue flashlight on each one in turn to see if they were legitimate, and finally satisfied, folded them neat and put them in his back pocket.

I started to push past him and he held his arm out to stop me. I wanted to break it in half.

"What gives?"

"You still aint getting in."

"What about the hundred bucks."

"That's for wasting my time. I'm a busy man."

This guy really likes messing with people, and with his size probably gets away with it most all of the time. I took a deep breath and sighed, then looked around for any potential witnesses to the crime that was about to happen. A couple of young Asian guys who'd also been denied entry were leaning against a railing nearby watching the scene unfold.

"You know I've seen a lot of messed up characters in my day, but you take the cake pal," I said. "What happened, someone kick you out of the sandbox in Kindergarten? Block the drinking fountain so you couldn't quench your thirst at recess? Carrying that around with you all this time, and now it's payback? It's gotta be something in your developmental years that made you like this. So what was it?"

He took it all in, stone-faced and mute, and spit on the ground.

"I'll tell you what," he announced. "If you can get by me, I'll let you in. I'll even give you back your hundred bucks, how's that?"

"All I have to do is get by you?"

"Get a single inch by me and you're in."

"One inch?"

"That's all its gonna take pal. I'm gonna feed you to the animals out back, and keep your hundred bucks." He planted his feet, cracked his knuckles, and got ready to repel me.

I shrugged my shoulders. "Well, alright I guess it's worth a try. If I can't get by a fat slob like you, I don't deserve the hundred back. What's your training if you don't mind me asking."

He smiled, and I could see he was missing a front tooth. "Fifth degree black belt Taekwondo. You?"

"Tenth degree kick your teeth in."

Some guys laugh at a challenge, when it comes to the critical moment and it's time for fists to fly, some guys seethe and the anger simmer out of their skin. This guy was of the simmering demeanor. His brow furrowed, eyes narrowed and turned red at the corners, little specks of spit coming out of his mouth as he bellowed. "I'm gonna tear the crap out of you!"

I backed up a step, made like I was a

sprinter at the track ready to race, feinted left, feinted right then went straight at him and brought my rigid right hand from down deep and karate chopped him on the neck, right at the L-18 ligament.

It was like I was karate chopping a concrete wall. This guy was built like a brick shit house with extra mortar in the cracks.

He grabbed me by the neck with both hands trying to squeeze the life out of me while kicking and kneeing me from below with fifth degree black belt moves.

I reached down and pulled out the buzzer from my pants pocket, pressed it against his forearm and lit him up with fifty thousand watts, and he turned into a human pin ball machine on tilt, the eyes in his head rolled around a couple of times and he flopped back on the concrete, white as a sheet and out cold.

"I don't play fair," I whispered into his ear as I grabbed him with one hand by the front of his belt buckle and the other by the back of his hair and dragged him into the bushes.

I glanced over at the two guys leaning against the railing, they were smiling from ear to ear, and obviously very pleased with what had just happened to the bouncer.

"Mind if we go in too?" One of them ventured.

I shrugged my shoulders. "Be my guest." They jumped at the offer and jogged towards the entrance in front of me, and I followed them in through the double doors.

It was dark and dingy and crowded at the

bar. It was basically a big warehouse sized room fifty feet by fifty feet, with a long bar on the left side of the room as you entered, and a stage on the right side with tables and chairs set up in between. A sharp rancid smell like sweat mixed with stale beer and booze and cigarettes and pot wafted through the air while a monotonous back beat drum solo accompanied by a dreadlock rapping gangster wannabe waltzed around on stage with his pants half way down around his skinny ass showing his underwear with his hat on sideways, pointing at the crowd now and then with two fingers like a gun barrel, boom boom pah, boom boom pah. I knew I'd finally arrived.

Well, I thought. They sure named the place correctly. The Pit. It smelled like an armpit.

I saw an open space near the end of the bar where the waitresses picked up their orders and walked over and sat down.

"What do you want?" The toughest looking bartender I'd ever seen asked me. Tattoos running up and down his arms and circling around his neck, religious quotes and voodoo skeletons, crosses and people's faces, flowers and daggers, hearts and bullets all rolled into one.

It was apparent to me right off the bat that we weren't going to get along, but I tried to be nice.

"Scotch and soda, hold the scotch." I told him.

"What are you a wise guy? Scotch and

soda's seven fifty, with or without the scotch." He grabbed a glass, filled it with ice and soda from the soda gun and set it down in front of me without a smile. "Seven fifty."

This had to be the most unsociable place I'd ever been to, but I needed info and thought I'd be a good guy as long as possible. I pulled out a ten spot, slid it onto the bar in front of him. "Keep the change."

He frowned and grabbed the money, changed it in the register, threw the tip in a big jar at the back and went down to the other end of the bar. There was a mirror lining the back of the bar where the glasses were stacked, and I could see the wood stock from a sawed off shotgun a couple of seats over and under the bar from where I was sitting.

Like the wild-wild west.

I had about five minutes to see what I needed to see, before the bouncer woke up and came looking for me, and I got busy and took it all in. Lining the walls were pictures of performers standing with some guy in a suit and gold chains. In every picture was the same guy with a suit and chains.

"How you doin' sweetie, haven't seen you in here before."

It was a study in contrasts, one of the toughest looking bartenders I'd ever seen was behind the bar, and yet here was one of the most stunning waitresses I'd ever seen in my life in front of it. Short curly brown hair and big round brown eyes made for melting a guy on the spot, and eyelashes made for cooling him down into an immovable object. Slim and taut and pert were the words that instantly came to mind. Perky, very perky was another analogy that seemed about right. She smiled, and it was just about the easiest thing in the world to smile right back at her.

"Yep, it's my first time here," I said, as steady as I could manage. "I heard a lot about this place and thought I'd give it a shot."

She emptied her tray that was filled with empty bottles and glasses and napkins, and counted out her money while keeping one eye on me. "Well, you can sit right there all night sugar."

"Say, who's the guy in all the pictures on the wall with the suit and gold chains. Is he a famous rapper?"

She looked at me with shock on her face. "Why that's Mr. Charles Washington the second. C-Dub's his nickname. He's not a rapper, he's the owner. This is the first club he opened, and he comes back every once in a while just for old times' sake. He's a real big shot now though. A billionaire."

I saw the star that I'd lost, Gale Nighting in one of the pictures with C-Dub. They were standing on the red carpet at some big event, obviously not in front of this club. "Hey, check it out," I said to my hot waitress. "There's that girl that got kidnapped."

She glanced over to the picture and frowned while shaking her head. "Poor thing, I hope they find her soon."

"Did she ever come in here?"

Her eyes scrunched up. “In here? You crazy? That girl has way too much class to come into a place like this.”

“Well, you’re here.”

She blushed, and the bartender came back from the other end of the bar and started making her drink order, crashing ice into glasses, pouring booze, popping the top off bottles of beer while looking sideways at me and said gruffly. “There’s a couple of tables up front pal, you should go sit there instead, you’ll be more comfortable and you’ll hear the lyrics better.”

“I kind of like it here, but thanks.” I turned back to the waitress. “Were you working here the night she got taken?”

“Who you talking about?” asked the bartender.

“Private conversation,” I warned him.

He got close to my face. “I thought I told you go sit somewhere else.”

She reached out and pulled his shoulder back. “It’s okay Bobby, he’s just making conversation.”

“What are you, a cop?” He asked me.

I shook my head. “I’m nobody.”

He scowled, then whispered low, “You got that right”, and finished her drink order and went back to the other end of the bar where a pack of thirsty animals were waving and yelling for him.

She got busy loading up her round tray with the drinks, arranging each glass and bottle nice and tight and uniform, taking her time and looking at me whenever she could. "I was working, yes. I work just about every night in here. Too many nights maybe." She glanced down the bar where the loud and tattooed one was slamming drinks on the bar for his buddies.

"Is that your boyfriend?"

She scoffed. "He wishes."

"He seems pretty jealous right about now."

"Well he should be with someone like you sitting here, sugar."

I looked deep into her brown eyes. "Call me sugar one more time and I might have to kiss you."

She smiled and leaned close over the bar. "Sugar."

Calling my bluff. I cracked and hesitated and she giggled at the sight of it. I wasn't so tough after all.

She picked up her tray and strictly advised me. "Don't you move, I'll be right back." Then walked into the crowd to deliver the goods.

My new best friend the bartender sauntered back down and posed in front of me, flexing his arms and generally scowling. He seemed pretty heated up this time around, clenching his right fist like he was ready to throw a punch at me.

Well I thought, I'd been here long enough and found out what I needed to know. The star never came in here, and wasn't expected that fateful night. Maybe the inside security team had kept it all a secret, and maybe she was headed here, and maybe she wasn't. The waitress told me everything she knew. I sure wasn't going to get any answers from this boneheaded bartender. He was trying to drill holes in me with his bloodshot and angry eyes.

"So what," I asked him. "Did they have a special at the tattoo shop? Buy one, get a hundred free?"

He leaned closer. "I'm just about ready to jump over this bar and beat the crap out of you."

It was the second time in past fifteen minutes I'd heard something like that. I shook my head. I'd had just about enough of this guy.

"All I hear is yap, yap, yap like a little Chihuahua. I don't think you could jump over a penny laying on the ground. What I've found in my life, is that having a tattoo doesn't make a guy tough. A lot of times, guys get tattoos to make themselves *seem* tough, to themselves, and to others. Mostly to seem tough to themselves though. It's kind of a lack of self-esteem issue. They get a tattoo to build themselves up mentally, to meet the challenges that face them throughout the day, kind of like a shield, or a mask to hide them from the harsh reality of everyday life. With the amount of tattoos that you have, I'd say you have issues."

He pulled a deep breath into his flaring nostrils slammed his fist on the bar and yelled. "That's it!"

I had my hand on the buzzer, ready to put it into action again, when there was a commotion at the front entrance. The bouncer staggered in holding a large handgun and people started moving away, scattering. Someone shouted GUN and the music stopped. This was not looking good.

"YOU!" he shouted and pointed the gun at me from about twenty feet, it had a long barrel and he was holding it with both hands to keep it steady. I was trapped. I looked over at the bartender and he was long gone, the tough guy scurried away pretty fast down to the other end of the bar.

I moved quickly to the right and jumped over the bar. Two pops from the pistol, screaming from the crowd, the mirror at the back of the bar shattering, all at once sounds, my quick breathing as I crouched behind the ice well and stinking bottles of booze, the wooden handle of the double barrel shotgun at eye level, and I pulled it out and checked the twin barrels, it was loaded and I aimed it at the ceiling over the entrance and pulled both triggers.

Very loud, a sawed off shotgun has a wide range of pellet splatter and at this range it hit the ceiling with a fifteen foot wide circle of destruction which rained down on the bouncer and gave me an opening. I pulled out my pistol, peered over the bar and squeezed off a couple of shots at his ankles and he went down. Again.

He was yelling and writhing in pain but still had his handgun and was firing wildly. The ceiling, the walls. The crowd had mostly scrambled out the back with a few stragglers trying to get through the door, and I saw my waitress waving me to come that way. I didn't hesitate and ran to the end of the bar and leaped over it, zigzagging around tables and chairs that were strewn about as though a pack of elephants had stampeded through. A pack of wooly mammoths like the old days. I pushed her through the door and followed her out into the black alleyway. Sirens wailing in the distance. I had to get out of here.

Bob Marley said one time that the biggest coward is a man who wakens a woman's love with no intention of loving her. I had no intention of loving her, but I did promise her a kiss and I owed her at least that much for getting me out the back door of the rap club.

I pulled her close and pressed my lips against hers and she did not resist, in fact it was the opposite, she held my shoulder, wanted me to linger but I pulled away and ran. The cops were coming and I had to get out of there fast. I followed some people who looked like they knew their way around these back alleys. Down and around the corner, I looked back for an instance and felt a stinger in the back of my leg, right above my knee and I stumbled. Felt like I'd been stung by a wasp, then it went deeper like someone stabbed me with an icepick. I'd been shot.

Back by the entrance stood the tattooed bartender with a small handgun, smiling. He knew he'd gotten me. I kissed his girl and he shot me, the bastard.

I could still walk, and walk I did. Steadily, heading as far and as fast as I could away from that place without drawing attention. I headed East towards Wilshire boulevard, following a like-minded group of rap club getaways. We all put our heads down and our hands in our pockets as the cop cars raced by, the occupants checking us out as they sped by. We weren't trouble makers, no sir just average citizens out for a stroll after a shooting spree in the ghetto.

The group ahead of me looked back and recognized me as one of the shooters in the bar, and they slowly crossed the street and angled away from me. When we got to Wilshire they went north and I went south.

I flagged a cab down and climbed in the back without letting on that I was injured. I was bleeding and could feel the warm sticky stuff in my shoes and running down my leg.

"How you doing tonight mister?"

"Fine," I lied. "Take me to Bell Plaza please." It was two blocks from my nurses apartment. I needed help. I was bleeding on the taxi seat and he would find out about it after letting me out. I figured if I got out at the plaza and walked the two blocks to her apartment, he wouldn't be able to track me down. Traffic was light at two in the morning and it took about fifteen minutes to get to the Plaza. I paid my fare and literally slid off the seat and out into the night. Waiting until the cab was out of sight I limped past the bus stop and into the apartment complex. Taking the steps one at a time and pausing with both feet at each one I finally made to the second floor landing and knocked on her door.

One second stretched into two, two to four and I needed to sit or lie down. I blinked my eyes hard and tried to stay awake.

Maybe she wasn't home. Maybe I was at the wrong door, maybe she had company. Too many maybes.

Feeling very woozy now, when the door opened she was a fuzzy blur, an outline of a person and she was asking me a question, but I couldn't understand what she was saying. I was having a hard time focusing my eyes, and I tried to say something, anything but my mouth wouldn't work, I was like a guppy out of water, my jaws gaping, gulping at the thick air, and everything went dark.

13.

The CCTV image was black and white and a little blurry with the low light. The head of the agency, Mason Takegawa and the head of the police department sat in the police chiefs office and watched it again.

"Is that your guy?" asked the chief.

"Sure looks like him, play it again. Damn, why can't they make a surveillance camera in HD?"

On the screen was the scene outside the entrance to the club looking towards the street. The bouncers back was to the camera and he had his hands around someone's neck, and then he's flopping around and falling backwards on the concrete.

"See that object in the perps hand? Portable juicer."

They watch as the perpetrator throws the bouncer into the bushes, then the tape jumps to inside the club, from the center of the bar over the mirror looking towards the entrance.

They watch as the bouncer enters the bar holding the gun, then pointing it and shouting, and people running everywhere, the perpetrator who threw the bouncer into the bushes is now being shot at. He leaps over the bar and grabs the shotgun, fires it and the whole ceiling, lights and fans and all, come raining down on the bouncer, who is then shot in the ankles by the perp, and the screen goes blank.

"Want to watch it again?" asks the chief.

"Naw, I've seen enough. That's Badger alright, that's our guy. Why in the hell would he go to the rap club?"

The chief tapped his finger against his forehead. "Maybe he was thirsty and wanted a drink. Maybe he likes rap music at one the morning. Maybe he had a beef with the bouncer from the past, and he was there to settle the score."

"Maybe he was looking for the girl," said the head of the agency. "After all that's where we were escorting her to, when she was kidnapped. You got to admit he's got a lot of balls to go in there, with half the town looking for him."

"You see how he took out the shooter, the big bouncer? Twice."

"If I was that bouncer I'd think twice about going up against Badger again. Next time he might find himself dead. He only got zapped and shot in the ankles, he's lucky it was only that."

"There's one other thing," said the chief.

"We have surveillance of the back alley. This one is really dark and blurry and hard to see, but check this out." He rolled the tape and they could see the back of someone running who was about the same size and shape and wearing the same clothes as Badger. He stumbles as he's heading around the corner of the building and they see him look back and hold his leg. He froze the last frame on the screen.

"Look at the timestamp on the bottom of the frame." It read 01:36:08.

"Now look at this footage, from the back entrance that looks out towards the alley. The next sequence shows the bartender at the back entrance, holding a smoking gun and smiling. The chief froze the frame. It also read 01:36:08.

"He got nicked," said the head of the agency. "He's injured. That bartender deserves a medal."

"We'll check the local hospitals to see if anyone was treated for gunshot wound."

"Probably a waste of time, but might as well. I don't think Badger would risk a hospital. He's probably got something else figured out. Hell, I'll bet he takes out the bullet by himself with a pocketknife. My bet is that he's going deep underground for a while. We better call C-Dub. and let him know."

"He knows all about it. He's the one who gave us the surveillance tapes," said the chief. "He's pretty ticked off that his club got shot up by the guy who stole his girlfriend."

"Put out an award," said Mason. "Print up

the best image we have of this guy and put a price on his head. Ten thousand dollars, we'll pay it, and it'll be well worth it. Get it to all the newspapers and local TV stations. Someone saw that guy. We'll find him."

14.

Charles H. Washington II sat brooding in the back of the limo as it made its way silently through the dark streets of the inner city. Whenever life took a turn for the worse and seemed a little tenuous, he liked to take a trip down memory lane to refresh his sense of being, his sense of self-worth. The past few days were draining on him, the events weighing him down. The limo stopped outside a dilapidated and worn tenement building, grey and cold in the middle hours between midnight and dawn, and the driver looked into the rear view mirror.

"Should I pick you up at the same place Mr. W, in an hour as usual?"

"That will be fine Carl." He got out of the limo, and straightened his overcoat, tapped on the top of the long car and watched as it sped away. This is where it all began, for him, the ghetto, where he was born on the street long ago. He checked the Glock 44 in his pocket, the cast stainless steel handle crosshatched for comfort felt reassuring to his hand, the silencer was tightened onto the barrel just right. This was very dangerous place to be at this time of the night, and he walked straight into the nearest dark alley, looking for trouble.

It didn't take very long. Up ahead in the darkness he could see the glow of a lighter and a pipe, and a couple of crackheads gathered around it, taking turns sucking off the smoky venom emanating from the end of it.

Demons, twisted and lost. As he got closer and they sensed his presence, they conspired among themselves to rob him. Whispering to each other in hushed tones they made their plans. He had on a nice new overcoat after all, he must be rich.

They spread out and blended into the shadows to wait for his passing, one grabbed a knife, another a long steel pipe from the gutter. The third and most ruthless held a cord of rope in which to throttle the rich guy.

C-Dub calmly pulled out the Glock and shot them all methodically and silently. Two shots each, once in the abdomen and once in the head. When he was satisfied that they were terminated, he continued on his walk into the ghetto. Dogs barked here and there but he kept on through the night.

At the corner of the second block he spied a small group of men next to a lamp post. Four of them. Silent and wordless, they seemed to be waiting for something to happen. He waited in a dark doorstop and watched. A car pulled up and stopped next to the group, one of them reached into the car, an exchange took place, and the car took off down the road. The men counted the money and it changed hands between them. Then not long after, another car came slowly up to the lamp post and the same routine was performed as before, one of the guys reached into the car, an exchange occurred, and the car drove off, then they counted and changed the money between themselves again. It was an old fashioned corner drug store. Selling crack or heroin or whatever the client wanted.

Charles H. Washington II reloaded the Glock 44 one bullet at a time, and strolled down the boulevard towards the dealers. They eyed him suspiciously as he approached, and two of them put their hands in their coats. They were the muscle and obviously packing guns of their own.

C-Dub's eyes narrowed and he gripped the Glock in his overcoat and kept walking forward. His momma died of an overdose from a hit of crack from guys just like these, and he couldn't think of a worse form of animal. He stopped ten feet away and they all eyed each other.

C-Dub shrugged his shoulders. "I'm looking for a couple of hits."

"You got any money?" said the one who was doing the car exchanges, and he took a step forward. "It's minimum five for a hundred."

"Sure I got cash," said C-Dub and he pulled out a big wad of money with his left hand, it was thick and folded in half with a hundred dollar bill on the outside, and he held it up high in the air for all to see.

The whole group's attention went to the wad of money in the left hand and they missed the gun coming out with the right, and he shot them all quickly and methodically before the muscle guys could get their own guns out. Two shots each as before. One of them lay gasping for air, and somehow gathered the strength to throw a bottle that broke on C-Dub's leg, and he gave that animal a third bullet for good measure. Right between the eyes.

He walked quickly down the street keeping to the shadows and in the corner of his vision he could see someone watching from one of the windows above. They quickly ducked down under the windowsill, closed the drapes and turned off their lights.

Every now and then, when he felt the world closing in on him he took a walk down memory lane, into the ghetto where it all began. The police always thought it was gang related, these shootings and they could never find enough clues to pin it on anyone, besides it was the worst of the worst who were getting shot, the drug dealers, the animals in the street who preyed on people with their narcotics and poison. The dead still had big wads of cash and unused drugs in their pockets and it didn't take much to put two and two together. The police didn't put much effort into investigating the murders.

He was a billionaire vigilante, and it

brought him no real pleasure, but it did bring a measure of strange satisfaction, a heartfelt revenge for his mother, who got caught up in a web she couldn't seem to escape from.

An hour later he was at the other end of the ghetto, three miles of walking and the limo was waiting for him at the cemetery where his mother was buried. It was a simple graveyard across the street from the Catholic Church. Thirty years earlier it had filled up and stopped taking new inhabitants, and his mother was one of the last to be interred there. She was three rows in from the end He lay a simple white carnation on her grave, then got into the limo and drove away into the morning.

15.

When I woke up, I had that strange elephants on my eyelids feeling again, only this time I wasn't in a hospital bed. It was a bed alright, but in a semi darkened room, and the mattress was soft and smelled nice, not like hospital formaldehyde and bleach, more like flowers and perfume and a pretty girl.

Filtered light came through the curtains that fluttered with the breeze and I could hear kids playing in a nearby park or school. I tried to get up but my leg felt like it was in a vice and I remembered. I'd been shot. Bob Marley was right, don't awaken love in a woman unless you intend to love her, and definitely don't kiss her if her boyfriend, wanna be or not, is standing nearby with a gun. Somehow I'd made it to my nurse's apartment. My beautiful nurse Amber.

I could hear water running in the kitchen and I made another attempt to get up. Gritting my teeth and helping my injured leg with my hands interlocked under my calf so I wouldn't bend my knee, I was able to swing my legs over the edge of the bed and sit up. Blood rushed downhill out of my brain, there was a ringing in my ears, and I felt like I was going to pass out. I fought it and regained a semblance of independence and took a couple of deep breaths. After a few moments of stability, the cloud left my head and I could almost think straight again. But I had no idea what time of day it was, or even what day it was. I'd lost a chunk of my existence.

I was dressed in shorts and a t-shirt and my leg was bandaged above the knee, bandaged and holding in a ball of pain in the middle of my leg. I made the next move and stood up and steadied myself by holding onto the end of the four poster bed and started limping to the door. It squeaked when I opened it and she looked over from the kitchen, startled. She was wearing her hair up and a baggy t-shirt and shorts, just like me, we were like twinsies.

She started to smile and then frowned and rushed over to me putting her arm around my back and helped me to the chair next to the couch.

"You should take it slow, you've been out for a while."

"How long?"

"Well, you fell through my front doorway at around two in the morning and it's nearly nighttime now, so about sixteen hours."

"I had a little problem."

She whistled and shook her head. "Really now. If you call taking a bullet a little problem."

"Someone took a shot at me. You bandaged me up. You saved me. Again."

"I called a friend at the hospital, she took out the bullet and stitched you up. You lost a little bit of blood, and since we know your blood type from your last little visit to our hospital she brought along some plasma."

"*She* took out the bullet?" I narrowed my eyes. "A fellow nurse?"

"She's pre-med, almost a doctor. She actually jumped at the chance to operate on a real person, and don't worry she can keep a secret."

Then she smiled and narrowed her eyes at me conspiratorially "But you can't."

"What do you mean?"

"Keep a secret. We kept you sedated for the operation with sodium pentothal. You were pretty blabby."

"Oh yeah?"

"I kissed the girl and he shot me, Bob Marley. You babbled it over and over again till you fell asleep."

"It's from a song."

"I have all his albums. Me and Bob go way back."

"I shot the sheriff? Remember that song?"

"You're not a sheriff. And there wasn't a girl in that song either. Look Badger, I don't care if 'he' shot you for kissing the girl. It's actually kind of funny if you did, and he did."

"Getting shot aint funny Amber." I took a deep breath let out a sigh, and searched her eyes. There was no malice there. "Alright look, I owe you big, very, very big, so here's the whole story, take it or leave it, throw me out on the street if you want. I've got a weakness for girls like you with big brown eyes, and she called my bluff. I'm stubborn and prideful, and I tend to joke around a little too much, especially when things get tense which seems to be happening a lot lately. I'm in a lot of trouble and I don't know how to get out of it. I like being in control of the situation, no matter what that situation might be, but right now the situation is in control of me. I'm looking for answers and running into a stone wall."

"Yes, I kissed the girl and her boyfriend shot me from behind, but it sounds more loose than it really is. I went to the club because that's where we were heading with the star before she got kidnapped. I wanted to find out what the people who worked there knew, and it turns out they never, ever saw her there and didn't even know she was going to visit that night. None of which means a damn thing either way. A couple of tough guys got in my way and tried to rough me up, and here I am."

She bit her lip, seemingly missing most of what I had said and repeated my first line. "A weakness for girls like me with big brown eyes?"

I nodded and smiled. "Usually gets me in trouble."

"There's something you need to see." She grabbed the remote and turned on the TV and the DVR. "I recorded it for you. Your big night on the town made the morning news."

On the screen was an anchor newsman and on a pop up screen next to him was the black and white CCTV footage from the security cameras at the bar, the bouncer getting zapped and thrown into the bushes, me grabbing the shotgun and blowing out the ceiling. Like a rampaging bully. They showed the shotgun scene twice. I was an out of control madman with a shotgun.

Then there was a still shot of me that filled the entire TV screen, with my name in bold lettering at the bottom under the words: WANTED. Then in smaller letters below, 'Ten Thousand Dollar Reward for information leading to capture.' And then in smaller letters, 'Armed and dangerous.'

"You're a popular guy."

"I never realized how selectively presenting the news could skew public opinion till right now. They should have shown the part where the bouncer was trying to twist my head off before I zapped him, and then firing a pistol at me before I blasted the ceiling with the shotgun."

"So the bouncer is the girl's boyfriend?"

"No, that's another guy."

She laughed and I shook my head and looked at the floor in shame.

"Yeah, I made a lot of friends last night."

16.

Nine AM on a hazy morning at the top of the tallest building in the city.

C-Dub gazed at the computer screen that was filled with numbers and graphs, holdings and assets with his name on it. The graphs and numbers were flexing, changing and going up and down, stocks, housing prices, record sales, the myriad of graphs turning red when they edged down, and green when they were edging up. Going up and down, but mostly going up, edging higher and higher. At the top of the screen next to the word TOTAL and an equal sign was a ten digit number.

One thousand million dollars equals one billion dollars. It had a nice ring to it. One billion dollars, and he said it over and over a few times for good measure. Just saying those three words when they actually belonged to you made them kind of pop out with authority, and then roll off a person's tongue, the largesse of it all magnified by ego.

He'd read once that a billion single dollar bills laid end to end would circle the globe four times. Still it wasn't anything to gloat over. A billion dollars was chump change in some circles. Trump had ten billion, and *his* wad of cash laid end to end would circle the globe forty times. Four times around was peanuts. Still, Trump didn't own a professional basketball team, and very soon if everything went well, the name Charles Washington II would be a minority owner of one of the biggest sporting franchises in the world. Put that in your pipe and smoke it Trump.

Still, a billion was nowhere near enough, not by a long shot. He needed more.

The range of liquid cash, the operating funds fluctuated throughout the day and throughout the hours and minutes and usually ranged from fifty to seventy five million as payments were received and payments were made. In one hand and out the other, like anyone else, just on a bigger scale.

His mind wandered back to the billion dollar number, usually he wasn't this sentimental about the past, but he was at a certain turning point in his life where it made sense to think about how he got this far. Except for the seventy five million or so in liquid operating cash, it wasn't a billion in cash with his name on it that he could throw in the air and take a bath in, it was all in assets. Real estate, and restaurants, bars, entertainment, clothing lines.

The first million was easy, he almost fell

backwards into it with Kid Rapper and the number one single in the nation for a couple of weeks. The second million was way tougher, and so he formulated a plan.

If he could find one rapper hanging out in front of a tattoo parlor, a rap club should able to attract more talent, unknown talent that he could mold and shape and ride like a horse to the money store, so he used the proceeds to buy an abandoned warehouse across the street from the tattoo shop and transformed it into the Rap House, kind of like the House of Blues in New Orleans, but here in LA where rap started.

It turned out that running a club was lot tougher than he'd planned. Just to get it up and running took all the cash he scooped from Kid Rapper. He had to renovate the building and that took permits and contractors, a liquor license, live music license, kitchen license, parking license, business license, tax license, name license, health inspection, building inspection, and that's when he realized that the city government was the biggest racket in the world. Everyone had their hand out, legally, and you couldn't question them or they'd shut you down. Pimps and thieves and crack dealers had nothing on these guys.

And on top of that, you had to man the joint. You needed employees to staff the place and insurance up the ying yang for fire, flood, theft, contents, earthquake, liability, health, workman's comp, all necessary and required by the head city of Los Angeles racketeers. He was down to his last penny when the doors opened, but when they did open, the money flowed like a jackpot.

The place went off the charts, there was a city limit to how many people you could cram into the place and there was a waiting line around the block to get in, and they were netting five grand a day after expenses.

Things were a little rough around the edges in the beginning like any restaurant business, some of the first staff hired tried to scoop some of the profits here and there, taking cash for the drinks and putting it into the tip jar instead of the register, and if there were fights or violence the cops shut the place down and the bottom line suffered and so order needed to be installed and maintained on a primitive level, and it became known to one and all that you did not go to the Rap House and cause trouble, because you might end up missing or dead, or both.

That's why it was a little unnerving that the place got shot up last night, and made the morning news in such an unhappy manner. Something like that hadn't happened in a long time.

Still the lessons learned opening up the club proved invaluable for the empire he was building. Once you figured out how to allocate personnel and resources, you could look at tightening up the bottom line profit margin. The money, the cash flow. The moolah.

Five thousand per day, one hundred fifty thousand per month, turned into one point eight million dollars by the end of the year which was some serious cash, and he invested everything in more bars and restaurants, and within five years he owned ten restaurant bars outright which were generating fifty grand per day, eighteen million per year, and he took that cash and started investing in cheap apartment buildings.

The real estate market had been going down for a couple of years and it was a perfect time to pick up a lot of inventory. At that point in time, it seemed like a good idea to get as much floor space as possible, then renovate where needed like he did with the restaurants.

While running the clubs he ran the record label as a sideline, and signed a couple more hungry rap stars and then branched into the mainstream with hip hop and soul. The record company grew with the industry and pretty much ran itself for a while, and then they started merchandizing the talent with clothing lines and started pulling in more money.

Every penny he made went into buying more real estate, and that was another big headache that had to be learned first-hand. Renters were both a source of steady income and also a source of mental anguish. Cheap apartment buildings meant cheap tenants, people who trashed the places and ran off without paying the rent.

Being a landlord took a whole other learning experience curve, and he slowly and painfully learned that it was better to own a few nice pieces of real estate with wealthy, meaningfully employed tenants, than a bunch of dirty run-down tenement's that always needed repairs, with unemployed bums on welfare and worse.

He had a piece of all the essentials that made the world go around and around. People needed houses and food and diversions and they would always pay for it.

Build it, provide it, maintain it, and rake in the profits. Whether it was a tattoo parlor, a club with booze and music, or a high rise apartment building it was all the same. Profit margin. Invest and provide a service for profit. He had a staff of ten accountants working full time, plus the assistance of one of the top CPA firms in the country as a backup. The basic motto of the company was cash flow.

The number one priority of this day was liquidating assets to free up cash for the basketball team minority ownership purchase. It was going to take seventy five million and they couldn't tap into the working capital without putting the whole system in danger. It was going to have to come from within the asset base, and it wasn't going to be pretty. It had to happen fairly quick too.

The investment group tapped him to be the next minority owner, but they had timelines to meet, bills to pay. They just signed the number one draft pick in the lottery who was going to put them back into the playoffs this year, at a huge cost. They needed money, liquid cash flow right now. These opportunities didn't come along very often. If he couldn't come up with the cash by the end of the week they'd go to the next guy on the list.

A sweet voice came of the intercom. "Mr. W, he's here, should I send him in?"

"Yes please."

An impeccably dressed man in his mid-thirties walked through the thick double doors that were held open by his secretary. He wore a silver double breasted suit with a jet black tie and jet black shoes, blond hair neatly combed and trimmed, freshly shaved with no mustache, and carrying a thin black briefcase. He could be either a banker or a hitman, but at this particular moment was a high priced courier.

C-Dub was brief. "It's about time."

"The traffic was..."

"Let's have it," C-Dub cut him off and reached for the thin case. He set it down on the desk and flicked open the locks. "The most paranoid business owners I've ever met."

"They said it's their final offer."

"So they said." C-Dub picked up the papers and started reading through them. A deal this big couldn't be negotiated over the phone, or by sending any documents over the internet said the opposing player. Sometimes an old fashioned courier was the safest route they said, so he sent his right hand man to pick up the latest offer. The man in the double breasted suit relaxed a bit now that his package had been delivered, and he unbuttoned his jacket revealing a silver pistol in a holster under his armpit.

C-Dub looked up instinctively at the shape

of the gun on the periphery of his vision, the quick muscles in his arm ready to pull at his own gun if needed. It was loaded and within reach. Then he relaxed and kept reading, while thinking to himself that maybe he was a little too on edge.

Most of the stack of papers was legal mumbo jumbo, the first party to the second party, yada yada yada. He got to the most important part and read out loud.

"Sixty million up- front, another twenty million in two months. Seventy five percent controlling interest with the up-front money and one hundred percent control with the remaining payment."

He pushed the papers away. "I don't have a problem with their having a controlling interest with that much of a down payment on the investment, but I do have a problem with the up-front money. It's not enough. They're ten million short. I told them flat out I need seventy million, or there's no deal. What is it about those two little words 'seventy million' that they don't seem to understand?"

"Maybe they don't have it boss. Times are tough."

"Those greedy bastards have it all right. And more. They've been after my record company for years now. They know what's happening, they read the stats. We're booming. They started at fifty up front, and now we're at sixty. We're getting closer."

"You want to write up a counter offer for them boss?"

"I wouldn't waste the paper." He scrolled through his rolodex till he found the number he wanted and picked up the phone." Making a phone call with an ultimatum, now that's the old fashioned way.

The smart phone on the other end rang three times and a voice answered. "This is Conrad."

The infamous Conrad Jones, filthy rich multimedia pirate and entrepreneur, thief and outlaw and now multi billionaire. Made his first million the old fashioned way, by stealing it legally, pirating songs before it was outlawed and selling digital copies overseas, under the radar.

"Conrad, it's C-Dub"

The phone on the other end was muffled like a hand over the speaker while someone talked to the side. Then another voice came on the phone, the real Conrad. This guy was so paranoid he wouldn't even answer his own phone.

"This isn't a secure line," said the gruff voice.

"They don't exist anymore," said C-Dub, " didn't you get the memo? We're all being tapped, all the time, everywhere, so we might as well just relax and be ourselves."

"Did your courier deliver our offer?"

"Yes, and that's why I'm calling."

"We'd prefer to do it our way. With a courier."

"This won't take long. You agree to my terms and I'll send him back to you with a legal document ready to be signed. Okay?"

A long silence, and abruptly: "Make it quick then."

"Seventy million, up front, ten million down the road, whatever date you want. But I want the seventy large now."

"Our offer stands, as presented."

Trying to be a tough guy. "I'm going to send you a snapshot of my computer screen, so you know where the company is headed. We're clearing half a million per day and rising. Wait any longer and I won't need you, or your money."

"Don't send it to this phone..." he tried to interject.

But it was too late, C-Dub clicked onto the Bad Rap Records graph and took a snapshot of the intricate graphs, all green and rising, zooming in and filling the frame with his smartphone and hit the send button.

"We're up twenty five percent across the board in the past three days."

"I see," said the voice on the other end.

"Right now you're in the pole position for winning the company," said C-Dub "but that could change quickly."

"There's another offer on the table?"

"Isn't there always?" he lied.

"We'll have to move some things around to meet... your deadline," said the other end. "Send your courier back with the revisions and we'll see what we can do."

"I need to know by tomorrow morning," said C-Dub, and when Conrad tried to talk, C-

Dub merely hung up the phone. Now that's how it was done, he thought. My terms.

"I never thought you'd sell the record company," said the silver suit. "That was the first company you owned."

C-Dub glared at him. "Second. The tattoo shop was the first. And don't' worry, I won't get all misty eyed when it's gone. There's something else I want more right now, and selling the record company is the easiest way to raise the money quickly. I'm very fortunate that it's doing as well as it is right now, wouldn't you say? Besides, I can always start another record company, all it takes is some raw talent and a studio to record an album. The rest is just promotion. Nothing to it."

The silver suit could see the gears shifting and stood up, while C-Dub wrote on a sticky note that he attached to the stack of papers, clicked the briefcase shut and pushed it over to him. "Take this over to Allen and have him make the changes and courier it back across town to Conrad."

"Sure Boss."

"But first let's settle all this other business." He pulled a stack of papers over in front of him and started going through it. "Here's the building contract for the new apartment complex, make sure there's no loopholes for any of these contractors to get out at the last minute, I want these guys all locked in ironclad before we commit to the bank for the loan. How's your guy down at the planning department?"

"Rock solid."

"You paid him?"

"A hundred and fifty grand in an offshore account. He's good to go."

"What about the other guy, the one who was opposed to the project?"

"He disappeared on a fishing trip off Baja yesterday. Five miles out, rough seas, it's a sad old story. Poor guy fell off the boat, no trace of him, the crew said he was wearing some heavy clothes and got dragged under by the current. They called off the search this morning."

"Darn shame," said C-Dub "What about the new guy, the one who's taking his place?"

"He's on-board with us a hundred percent, we got him greased up and ready to go, like a fat happy pig on his way to the luau, apple in his mouth and all. He's got his own brand new offshore account and we put the first fifty grand as good faith into it. The mayor should be appointing him next week as soon as the official mourning period is over. Can't do these things too quickly you know. There's a certain protocol to follow."

"Of course. They need to bury the poor guy, in spirit if that's all they got before they can move on. As long as we got the new guy in there before the vote on the project goes to the panel. What about the widow?

"She's okay. Found out the husband was having an affair."

"Was he?" Asked C-Dub his eyebrows arching.

"Does it matter?"

C-Dub shrugged his shoulders. "Not to me it doesn't."

"She gets a nice fat insurance settlement, and doesn't have to deal with the lying cheating bastard anymore."

"Works for me," said C-Dub "Alright, that's that. Now the golf course problem needs to be solved. Who the hell do these guys think they are holding up the water rights?"

"It's a woman named Agnes Stillwater of all things, Stillwater can you believe it? She's on the water board and is throwing a monkey wrench into our request for extra treated water for the back nine, says it should be going to the farmland by the freeway bypass."

"We're in a damn drought and the back nine looks like hell lately, doesn't she realize people won't pay to play on a brown golf course? We have to get the course up to full speed before right away, they're making a decision on the PGA event, and I want that event, dammit. Maybe Agnes Stillwater can accidently drive herself off a cliff, or drop the hairdryer into the bath tub whilst taking a bubble bath. Stranger things have happened."

"I'll work on it. How's the NBA deal shaping up?"

C-Dub gritted his teeth. "We're almost in. They're giving me an extra week to come up with the cash and I'll finally have my little piece of the franchise."

"A little bit's better than nothing, right boss?"

"For now it is, all I need right now is to get

my foot in the door. I'll get in there and bide my time, enjoy the moment, make happy kissy face and be the good guy, and then when the other shareholders slowly fade away or die suddenly, I'll be there to console the survivors, and increase my share, till someday in the not too distant future, the team will be all mine."

The room was silent for a moment as they pondered the thought of it. And then C-Dubs wheels began to turn again. "You know what the most powerful thing in the world is?"

Bob Silver squinted and thought for moment then felt the metal object at his armpit. "A gun?"

"No"

"A nuclear bomb?"

"Nope."

Bob was stuck. What could be more powerful than a nuclear bomb?

"Love," said C-Dub.

Bob laughed out loud. "You're joking right? Love? That's the damnedest thing I've ever heard you say. You putting me on boss?"

C-Dub's face was rock steady. "Not just any kind of love though. There's all kinds of love out there, love for someone of the opposite sex, love of art, literature, love of a child or a parent or a sibling or a pet, or of nature or science or puzzles or hobbies and sports. But I'm telling you that's all kid stuff. For infants and babies and people whose minds are lost in la-la land. The most powerful love is the love of money."

Bob was silent, and C-Dub continued.

"We're talking power here, right? Total power. Control. You see with money you can buy anything in the world, guns, armies, weapons, people, nuclear bombs, even whole governments if you want, with which to control people, control the world. And if you love money, you will gain money, you will nurture it and grow it and protect it and use to gather more money."

"You're serious."

"Dead serious. I love money because of what it can do for me. I want to gather as much money as I can, as fast as I can, and anyone who gets in my way is gonna get rubbed out. Quickly. You ever heard of Alexander the Great?"

"Sure, the guy who conquered the world. He was great." Bob laughed at his own little joke.

C-Dub remained serious. "Sure he's remembered as Alexander the Great, and everyone instantly thinks good things of him, a unifier, a great general, a conqueror, a champion. Cities are named after him. Everyone likes a winner right?"

Bob shrugged his shoulders. "Of course."

C-Dub nodded. "Sure, everyone loves a winner. Alexander the Great conquered the world with weapons and armies and brutality. He destroyed whole cities who got in his way, butchered thousands of people and entire populations on any given day if they didn't surrender to his marching armies. After a ten year campaign of terror whole countries in his path surrendered rather than be obliterated. Word got around, the guy was ruthless. And he's remembered as Alexander the Great for his success, not for his murderous destruction. They could have named him Alexander the Annihilator."

"What's that got to do with the love of money?"

"How do you think he paid for his army to go rampaging across the world? And bought new armies on the way? Money. He ransacked the treasuries of all the cities and kingdoms he conquered and used it to plow his way across the globe sacking as he went. He loved money and it took him places, got him the results that he wanted. And when he was on his deathbed he told his assistants to take him to his grave with his pockets turned out and his palms facing up and empty to show everyone that he was leaving this earth with no money."

"That's a great story boss. So are you planning on conquering the world like that guy?"

C-Dub sat back in his chair and tapped his chin in reflection. "One step at a time Bob. One step at a time."

17.

Bulldog sat in the front seat of the non-descript black suburban town car with the tinted windows that everyone on the block knew was either a cop car, or an undercover cop car. He turned to his partner in the passenger seat.

"So I've been meaning to ask, have you ever actually erased anyone?"

"I'm getting ready to right now actually," said Jerry and checked the grip on his pistol.

"Because if it's just a rumor, I need to know. Being your compadre, your amigo, your right hand man on this mission I need to know if you got the right stuff, or got no stuff at all." Bulldog was still pissed about taking the heat for letting Badger get away from the hospital and he wasn't going to let Jerry forget about it.

They were sitting outside the Crown Plaza watching the traffic, the people, the whole scene go down. Earlier that morning a cab driver walked into the local police precinct and reported that he'd seen Badger, had in fact given him a ride from the scene of the crime at the club to this exact spot. He was angry when he found out that the back seat and floorboards were soaked in blood, ruined his car in fact, and when he saw the morning news and the picture of the wanted guy he decided to do his civic duty and report it right away. Plus he wanted the ten thousand dollar reward.

They watched as a marked police cruiser passed them by for the fifth time that hour, the two occupants in the front seat glowering at them as they had every previous time. The police were miffed that the protection agency got wind of the wanted guy's last known whereabouts and seemed to think that their investigation was being hindered by the black car sitting in the exact spot that the guy had last been seen.

"Those guys are blowing our cover," said Bulldog. "Beat it!" And he waved with the back of hand in the direction of the departing cop car.

Jerry looked over at his partner with disgust. "Blowing our cover? Everyone within a mile radius has us pegged as a narc. This is a damned waste of time. We need to either start driving around like those guys, or get out of the car and start walking around, asking questions, finding leads."

"Look at the way you're dressed," said Bulldog. "Black suit and tie you look like a detective, no one will tell you anything unless you have a warrant, and you 'aint a cop."

"We'll ask some kids if they've seen him around, they like cops. I'll flash my private eye license real fast, like it's a badge."

"They'll throw rocks at you," said Bulldog. He checked his watch. "It's nearly five o'clock, it'll be dark soon."

Private eyes, trained and true they both looked as one as a small car passed by with a very attractive brunette driving. She had her driver's side window down and her hair curled away from her face in the gentle breeze, piling onto her well-formed shoulders covered in a crisp white blazer. Their heads turned as she passed following her with their eyes. She kept her head straight ahead although it must have been apparent that they were staring at her.

"Nice Betty," said Bulldog.

"She's got it going on," said Eraser, then he whipped his head around again as it came to him, she was wearing a white uniform, he'd seen that face before. "That's the nurse from the hospital. I'm sure of it." He eyed the license plate and pulled a pen and notepad from the glove box and wrote it down.

"Maybe we should follow her," said the Bulldog.

"Naw, I got an idea," said Eraser. "She looked like she was heading to work. Looked like she just got in the car and was letting it air out a bit with the window down. I've got an idea she lives somewhere around here. This is just too much of a coincidence. We're staying right here. Her name is Amber, I remember that much." He got out his E-tablet and punched into the agency database system. Their set-up was *way* better than the cops. They could quickly search for anyone's phone, address, credit report and police record with just a name or a license plate. He could find out what color they liked, where they shopped, what their favorite food was, and look at their online media accounts, within seconds. He punched in the license plate number and the name Amber and her whole life unfolded on the screen. Single, divorced, twenty eight, height weight, medical records, pictures, bank accounts, credit cards, address.

"She lives at 2807 West Figueroa, apartment 3G. We're currently sitting at 2607 West Figueroa."

"That's two blocks from here," said Bulldog.

Eraser looked at his partner, his eyebrows arched. "That's a coincidence. What do you think the odds might be that he's shacking up with the nurse?"

18.

The phone in the apartment rang loudly five times slowly and methodically, ringing and ringing like it expected me to pick it up, and I just stared at it, a little light headed with a sore leg. I stayed put on the couch with my leg propped in the air on a bunch of fluffy pillows, and watched the phone in case it jumped off the kitchen counter and I had to catch it.

Then the answering machine clicked on and I could hear a generic greeting in a monotone robot voice. Amber was smart not to record her own voice I thought, too many weirdos in this world, might think she lived alone. And then her voice came on the recorder. It was agitated, and loud.

"Badger this is Amber, pick up the phone, pick up the phone, please pick up the phone. PICK UP THE PHONE!"

Alright,alright, what's the rush. I struggled to get off the couch. My name is Badger, but I feel like I'm the one *being* badgered. I hobbled to the kitchen and found the receiver and picked it up.

"Hi Amber, everything okay?" The medication they'd given me was lingering and my words came out as slow as molasses on a frosty morning.

"I don't think so Badger. As I was driving to work just now I passed a car with two guys sitting in it a couple of blocks from my apartment. They were staring at me, and I think they recognized me from the hospital. It's the two guys from the agency who were in the hospital room with you. One of the guys I'm certain is the one you knocked unconscious and put in the bed."

I thought as quickly as I could in my walled up mental state. A couple of blocks from here was where the cabbie let me out last night. He must have squealed when he saw the reward on the TV.

"How long ago did you pass them?"

"Two minutes. I went around a corner and pulled over to call you."

"I have to go. This is very important, now listen carefully, they'll be able to trace me to your apartment pretty quickly, so you can't come back here, you'll have to stay at a hotel or with a friend for a couple of days. Find a good lawyer, not a cheap lawyer, a good one and put him on a retainer, I'll pay you back. Tell him everything, the truth, the agency at the hospital drugging me up, I forced you to take me in that first night, and last night you took me in and helped me when I was hurt, it's your duty as a nurse, nothing more. Get it on paper in case you need it. I won't be back to bother you anymore and thank you for your help so far."

"Badger wait.."

I cut her off, hung up the phone and got dressed. It wasn't easy putting on my pants, I could barely bend my left knee and finally had to sit on the couch to accomplish the task. Guns, ammo, pepper spray, zapper, all tucked quickly away in pockets and holsters, grabbed the money and stopped for a millisecond to listen and plan. They were on their way. They might even be climbing the stairs right now. I pulled the curtain on the front window to the side, peered out and could see a shiny black car pull into the lot across the street and maneuver behind a wall.

There was a back glass slider door that opened out onto a small porch area, just big enough to put out a chair, and have a smoke or drink after work or read the paper and have a view of the city. It doubled as a fire escape and a metal ladder angled down from the side towards the lower floor. It looked rusty and untrustworthy, so I climbed on slowly and let myself down to the balcony below.

The slider on this floor was shut tight and the curtains drawn. There was a single chair and small table and the rest of the lanai was covered with potted plants like a mini forest. From here you had to physically lower the remaining ladder section to the ground below, and I got prepared to swing it down when I saw the movement at the corner of the building.

It was the Eraser, gun drawn and sliding around the corner and along the wall, all the while looking up at the third floor windows. I crouched, trying to make myself very small like the plants surrounding me. His partner must on the opposite side of the building doing the same thing, getting ready to climb the stairs stealthily and quiet and then kicking the door down.

I was trapped. I looked at the window that I'd just come from and was relieved to see that I'd closed it. Through a crack in the lanai I could also see Eraser cautiously looking up at the windows and counting in his head. He wasn't sure which window belonged to the apartment I'd been in. He inched along until he was just about under the lanai I was crouching on, and looking up at the next door neighbors lanai.

"A little bit closer buddy", I was whispering, "just a little bit to the side".

I peered cautiously over the railing and he was right below me, looking up at the wrong window, face turned away from me, so I slid my good leg over the railing and dropped down on top of him.

At the last split second he heard a small noise and whirled around and looked up just in the nick of time to see the bottom of my shoe meet his face with a *crack*. He broke my fall with his face, gun clattering to the side, and we crumpled to the ground with him piled under me and I heard him groan as I knocked the wind out of him.

He was wiry like a cat on his back and tried to twist up and out from under me. Dust rose in a heap around us as he tried to push me off, and I gave him a short left hook to the chin, and karate chopped him on the L-18 ligament for good measure. I checked his pulse, still alive, neck not broken, but out cold. I looked through his pockets and grabbed his wallet from his pocket, and his gun that was laying on the side, and scanned the perimeter.

A couple of kids had been playing in the empty scrub filled lot next door, and they were now looking straight at me, eyes wide with fear at the sudden violent action. I put my index finger to my lips in the universal 'be quiet' signal. Their mouths were hanging open and as soon as they realized I was looking at them, they turned and hightailed it out of there. I followed suit, but in the opposite direction.

I looked back and up at Amber's third floor balcony, but saw no movement at the slider. The other guy was probably taking his time getting into the apartment, thinking that the back escape route was covered. He was wrong. When I got to the corner of the building I peeked around and saw a row of dirty metal trash cans and dropped the gun into the first one, put the wallet in the second, and headed for the street, and patted the dust off my pants as I walked.

In the rush of the moment I'd forgotten that I had an injured leg and as I strolled calmly towards the street I had to physically offset the pain to keep from limping. I didn't want anything about me to make people look at me, to recognize me from the picture on TV. I needed to blend in. I pulled the baseball cap lower and angled my head towards the ground, and stood waiting on the curb and waved down the first cab I saw. He pulled cautiously to the curb and I gingerly slid into the back seat and was instantly polite and well-spoken with an Australian accent.

"Thanks mate, good on ya to pick me up. Nice town you got here. Ows about taking me to the center of town so I can ave a look around?"

He was a middle aged Chicano, Myles Rodriguez read the license over the front passenger seat. Chicano with a born and bred SoCal accent.

"The center of town? That's a five mile wide area buddy, can you be a little more specific?"

"Anywhere near the center is fine mate, I'm just here on 'oliday, havin a look around is all. No worries."

"Aussie?"

"Yeah right, Melbourne. First time in the states mate. First class town you got here, lots of pubs and friendly people I'd say."

He shook his head. "Depends on where you go I guess. Some parts aren't so nice pal. I'd stay out of Compton if I was you."

"Why, don't they like tourists out that way?"

"Sure, they like 'em well enough I guess. They eat 'em for breakfast. Fried, roasted, raw, doesn't matter. They'll chop you up and put you in a blender for a smoothie."

I could see him trying to get a better look at me in the rear view mirror and I kept my face turned to the side while looking out the passenger window. I needed a car, a used one, the kind a school teacher or a nun would drive. Small, non-descript and blend-in-able. Somewhere on this route there would be a used car dealership. Public transportation was getting too dangerous and I needed to be mobile.

"So what," he continued. "Are you like that crocodile guy in the movies, here on a walkabout?" He looked in the rear view mirror again trying to pin me down. "Are you part aborigine or something?"

Why couldn't I get a cabbie that minded his own business? This guy was so chatty he should be a barber or a bartender. He thought I was a tribesman from the bush, and I rubbed my cheek and looked at my hand, maybe I had dirt on my face from my scramble back there with the Eraser.

"Yeah, might be some of the wildness in there from an ancestor or two, you never can tell mate." I kept up the small talk to keep him too busy to look at me, keep him driving and talking rather than driving and checking me out. I couldn't blame the taxi driver from last night ratting me out to the cops, but I didn't want it to happen again. "What about you mate?" I asked him. "Are you a Native American?" Throwing him a curveball.

He laughed and then seemed offended. "No, I'm not an Indian buddy. Do you even know what an Indian looks like? I'm fifth generation Chicano, man. My Great Grandpa came to California in nineteen oh one to work in the oil fields right back there in La Brea where I picked you up. Those were boom times man, and he never left. Picked up a wife and started a family. A big family, ten kids. And those ten kids all had ten kids and so on. We're Rodriguez, from Michoacán., but we're Americans now through and through, and we're everywhere in the city pal. Look up the name Rodriguez in the phone book and there's about twenty five pages worth. You can't hardly throw a rock in a crowd without hitting one of us. But I wouldn't recommend it." He held up his fist and shook it as a warning.

Up ahead on the left side of the boulevard I could see thirty foot tall flagpoles with brightly colored flags waving in the wind, ten of them in all with the words alternating: Sale, Autos, Buy. Not very subliminal, but very effective. They got my attention. I made sure the driver couldn't see my eyes as I looked at the lot as we passed. I barely glanced at it but took it all in like a high speed camera. There were over a hundred cars in the lot squeezed in from every angle. Big cars, little cars, shiny cars and dull ones. I waited until we'd gone a couple of blocks and I told him to pull over. I could tell he was a little disappointed and wanted to talk to his new Aussie friend some more. I handed him a twenty and told him to keep the change and he gave me a business card in return.

"Call me if you need another ride, okay? And remember, stay out of Compton. Say, you never told me your name. What kind of name do Aussie's have anyways?"

"Kelly's the name, Peter Kelly. My ancestor was a prisoner from Ireland sent to colonize Australia in the 1700's, and he never left either. Bloody oath mate, you can throw a slab into a crowd and hit a Kelly. Funny world."

He was puzzled. "What's a slab?"

"A pack of beers." I took the card, closed the door and watched as he sped away into traffic, and sure enough, there on the back of the yellow taxi, emblazoned in neon pink was the word 'Rodriguez'.

19.

As soon as the taxi was well out of sight I doubled back to the car lot and crossed the street. It was empty, no customers today which made it perfect timing for me. A trailer sized office set on pilings was on the side of the lot with a staircase leading up to the door which was closed. A big sign above the door read OPEN. Floor to ceiling windows lined the front of the building and they were glazed with a silver reflective coating. Guaranteed someone was in the building standing in front of one of the windows, and looking out at me right now. Sizing me up, looking me over, figuring out the angle he was going to take on selling me a car right here and right now. Whoever it was, he didn't know how easy he was going to have it. I surveyed the scene for a couple of minutes as I walked, then stopped in front of a nice suburban van and kicked the front tire and peered into the driver's side window. I tried the door but it was locked. What the hell, this wasn't the car I wanted anyways but I wanted someone to come out and show me around. I had five thousand dollars burning a hole in my pocket and I needed a car right now.

I saw the one I wanted, had it picked out even as I walked across the street. On the back row, tucked into a corner, a small white passenger car practically hidden by the tall SUV's around it. It was downright insignificant in appearance, dull, neutral and boring, no one would ever want to look at it twice. If it ran it was perfect. Finally, I saw in the reflection of the car window, behind me the office door swung open and out strolled a slick salesman, late middle aged, around forty eight or fifty years old I estimated, straightening his tie and cinching up his slacks as he made his way down the stairs.

"How're you doing today?" he asked with a wide smile, white teeth gleaming in the glare of the overhead lights, with his hand out. "Bob is my name, they call me big Bob, glad to meet you."

I shook his hand. "How do, name's Tex Parker. Mighty fine lineup ya got cheer."

He took a step back and whistled. "You from Texas, that how you got your name?"

"Yessir," I said. "Born and raised in the Lone Star state. Got transferred here yesterday for my job in the phone company and I need a vehicle."

"Well you came to the right place son. And just in time too, I reckon." An old salesman trick, mirroring his customer's traits, trying to make like he was a hick like me. "I noticed you limping a little when you was walking up here, time to get you off your feet and into a nice ride."

Damn, he noticed my limp. "Yep," I admitted. "I'm used to wearing cowboy boots, but they got me wearing these here city slicker shoes and I'll be damned if I got me a couple of blisters the size of Dallas."

He laughed at that and put his arm around my shoulders and maneuvered me over to the row of trucks. "One of these will make you feel right at home young man. As you can see, these are Texas sized trucks, V-8, four by four, lifted, fat tires and rims, and ready for action, son."

The guy smells like gin and I think if he calls me 'son' one more time I might have to bust his lip. I flexed my knuckles just in case.

He continued on. "Now, all our vehicles are inspected by a top notch mechanic at an independent facility, and are virtually free of any defects, mechanically or otherwise. You can rest assured that when you buy a car from big Bob, you can rest at ease. Now which one of these trucks do you want to test out?" He smiled at me hopefully.

I shook my head. "None of 'em. I have to drive long distances for my job and I need to have good..., no make that great gas mileage. I'm a conservative." I pointed to the car I had picked out. "How much for that little white car sitting back there?"

He grimaced. "That car?" He was sorely disappointed. His commission was going down by the minute. "You don't want that car son, it's...it's." He was at a loss for words. "It's not a very manly car to be blunt. That car is made for a little old lady, bottom line. You heard the saying about the little old lady from Pasadena? Well that's her old car, she traded it in cause it made her look too old." He smiled and was having fun with me, but I was in a hurry and it was time to take him down a notch.

I took a step back with a serious demeanor and sized him up. "What are you trying to say about my taste in a vehicle? Do you want to sell a car today or not?" Bluffing that I was pissed off.

He took a deep breath and sighed. "You're right, you are so very right. My apologies sir. It's priced at a very affordable two thousand five hundred, and gets great gas mileage. Why don't we take it for a test ride?"

I smiled, "now you're talking."

He started it up and pulled it out for me then jumped in the passenger side and I drove it around the block. It pulled to the right a little and had squeaky brakes, but seemed pretty solid. "You got a deal," I told him.

Back at the office I peeled off twenty five hundred dollar bills and laid it on the table. He filled out the transfer paperwork. "Now I just need to see your I.D."

I pulled out the Texas driver's license with my fake name Tex Parker on it and slid it across the desk. He looked at the picture and then at me. "Can you take your sunglasses off so I see your eyes?"

"What do you want to do that for?"

"Regulations."

"You have to see my eyes to sell me a car? The lights hurt my eyes, that's why I'm wearing sunglasses. I had surgery a couple of days ago. That's me, right on the license, you can tell."

He seemed a little unsure, hesitant. And that's when I saw the newspaper sitting on a pile behind him and on the front page was a frame grab from the bar with me holding the shotgun and getting ready to blow out the ceiling.

I needed the car and had to roll with the punches this time. Sure I could knock him out and tie him up till I got far enough away, but what if he wasn't even suspicious of me and this really just standard procedure and what he was required to do when he sold a car. Maybe I was just being paranoid.

"Alright," I said and took off my sunglasses and squinted. "Satisfied?"

He smiled. "Why thank you son, here's your paperwork and the key to your new car, you're all ready to go."

When I drove off the lot I knew he was probably phoning the cops so I headed straight East towards the civic center and found the nearest hardware store and bought a long sleeve shirt and rubber gloves, masking tape, a newspaper, ten cans of black metal spray paint and a screwdriver.

I was parked in the darkest corner of the lot and quickly switched plates with the car parked next to me. Then I drove around the block and found a dark alley between two apartment buildings, parked behind a dumpster, taped off the bumpers, headlights side mirrors and windows with the newspaper, put on the shirt and gloves and methodically sprayed the cans of paint and within ten minutes I had a black car. Pulled the tape and newspaper, rolled the mess into a ball and tossed it in the dumpster, then jumped in and backed out the way I'd come. It was a ten minute pit stop, and now I had a black car.

I zigzagged through the city streets, down one block, over two, down two blocks over three, until I was certain no one could be following me. Then back onto Wilshire and headed to the city again.

Flashing police lights up ahead, three cars boxing in a small white sedan like the one I'd just bought, five cops had the driver, a guy wearing a baseball cap spread eagled on the front bumper. Hands behind his head, face down on the hood. One cop was frisking him while another held a flashlight in the suspects face. Thought they had me. Traffic was backed up as everyone rubbernecked what was going on, and when I slowly passed by the scene, not one of the cops paid me any notice. They were looking for a white car and mine was as black as the night that had descended onto the city. Still, I turned my face as I passed by not wanting to take the chance.

That bastard at the car dealership sold me a car and then ratted me out, just as the cabbie had done last night. It was like the whole city was against me. Greedy bastards turning against their customer, someone who paid them honest money for a product or a service, and then backstabbing them, turning them in to the authorities to reap a tainted profit. Like Judas.

And even though I wasn't anything remotely near to the Christ Jesus, it was the same sort of betrayal. I was innocent of any crime. So far anyways, but that might change if I kept getting backed into a corner. Didn't these city people know you weren't supposed to back a badger into a corner?

So far I'd been a nice guy, reserved even by my standards. Sure, I had to knock a couple of guys out, fire a couple of weapons, but the only one who got seriously injured it seemed was me. I was tired of being hunted. It had been three days now, and I was going to run out of steam. The police seemed to be clueless with this case, this crime. Chasing after the wrong guy, me. I was being set up, the fall guy, the patsy. Somewhere the real culprit was laughing. It looked like it was up to me and me alone. I had to find the star, without any help from anyone, this is how it was shaking out, and was without a doubt the only way out of this mess. Find the star, solve the crime and get the cops and the agency and the whole city off my back. But I didn't know where to start.

I had point A and point B and that was it. Her house and the club and the place in between where someone nabbed her.

The place in between where someone

nabbed her...

The traffic light. Someone was able to switch the lights after I passed through, stopping the convoy and attacking them before I could get back to them.

The light switch was easy, you could buy one on the black market and it would be untraceable. There was no line there.

I had to go back to the scene of the crime again. Maybe talk to the Chinese dude in the restaurant. He told me not to come back again, but I had no choice. I pulled a U-turn and headed back to Bell and Crenshaw.

It was eight o'clock when I found a place to park, two blocks away. It never varied. Two blocks was always a good number, far enough away to avoid detection and close enough to run at a clip and escape the way you came. I put on a beanie and overcoat and locked my new car. Like the Chinese guy had said the first time I was here, it's a dangerous neighborhood.

I walked down the same side of the street that the restaurant was located on, so I could observe the opposite side and when I got to the corner I lingered and found a darkened doorway to hang out in. The restaurant looked busy enough, cars parked on both sides of the street, people streaming in and out, sometimes with square white carry-out boxes. Business was good. The rest of the block was dark and deserted. The building across the street from the restaurant was boarded up with a big shiny 'For Sale' sign on it with a national real estate firm. It was a two story brick building, looked solid enough for a sniper, the brick walls would deaden the sound of the pop, the top floor had windows every ten feet or so, like an apartment building with individual rooms. It was the only two story building on that side of the street, the rest were one story cracker box stores, one selling used appliances and crack seed, a guitar shop and a dry cleaner.

Whoever shot me off the bike either had to crouch on top of one of the single store buildings, or did the deed from one of the boarded up second floor windows. My bet was a second floor window. There's no way they could get a good shot off from inside a parked car. Too many witnesses at ground level, plus the difficulty factor of a tight space and a moving target.

I dialed the number on the sign, maybe someone would still be working at the real estate office, but no such luck, and all I got was a recording. I wanted to find out who owned the building, who had access. It was a long shot, but at this point in time everything was a long shot. Except for the sniper shot that took me off the bike. It was only about thirty feet from one of the windows to the street where I would have been riding, blasting it back to the intersection, and then crashing headlong into the empty building next to the restaurant.

I walked across the street and down the alley next to the boarded up building and found a side door. It was locked with a deadbolt on the inside, and I found an old newspaper in the trash piled up against the brick wall, waded it around my fist and punched out the glass in the center of the door, and reached in and unlocked it. It was musty and dusty inside and I closed the door and clicked on my pen light to find the stairwell tucked into an alcove by the front door.

There was dust everywhere which was going to make my investigation easier. The center of the stairway steps had less dust than the edges which indicated that they had been used recently. It didn't mean a thing as the realtors selling the property might have taken people up and down the stairs to show the place.

At the top of the stairway was a long hallway and five doors, all open and I went into the first room. A large rat scurried across the floor and into a closet. I followed it with the pen light and could see it disappear into a hole at the baseboard. The place was a pit.

The windows were boarded up from the inside with half inch plywood and deck screws. The plywood was cut straight and clean and was the best thing about the place so far.

I scanned the floor in front of the window. It was covered in thick white dust and three pronged rat foot prints with pointy little claws at the tips of the prints, cobwebs hung from the edges of the plywood. I looked at the centers of the deck screws, the triangle edges were clean as though they were installed by a pro with no stripping. I had to keep from sneezing from all the dust, and as I went into each room I saw the same thing, thick dust and rat prints, and plywood, except for the last room, the one on the corner that looked towards the restaurant. Thick dust and covered in footprints again, only this time they were human.

The area in front of the boarded up window looked like someone had a soccer match, the footprints were facing every which way and there was a totally clean area in front of the left corner, someone wanted to get a good foothold on solid wood. No cobwebs on the corners of the plywood, and I looked at the centers of the deck screws, some were stripped and mangled as though they were taken off and re-attached with the wrong size screw-bit by an amateur. This is where the sniper stood, or crouched.

I searched the floor for evidence, a bullet casing, a hair, piece of skin, anything. But there was only dust and footprints. Time to move on.

I let myself out the way I came in and walked down the alley and kept to the shadows and watched the restaurant for a while. It was nearing ten o'clock and the crowd was thinning out. I could see the old man helping with dishes and my friend the young Chinese guy talking to some customers at the cash register. The last time I saw him he ushered me out the back way, and told me not to come back. I don't listen very well.

He didn't seen me at first when I walked up the steps and through the doors, he was still busy talking to the customer at the cash register, there was something wrong with the credit card the guy was trying to use, and neither one of them seemed pleased. Finally the customer pulled out another card, which must have been the magic one, since they both smiled as the machine sprang to life and sputtered out a strip of paper. They shook hands and the customer went out through the doors and as the Chinese guy looked over at me sitting at a nearby table his smile melted into a frown. He semi-shouted something in Chinese to the old guy and strolled over to me while wiping his hands on a towel hooked into his belt and stood in front of me with a scowl that seemed to come from the other side of the planet.

"You don't look too happy to see me again," I said.

"I tell you never come back here, but you don't listen. No, you don't listen."

"Yeah, I don't listen very well. It's a problem I've had since I was a kid. My old man always said I had a hearing problem."

"You're gonna have more than a hearing problem if you don't get out of here. I saw you on TV. You're big news buddy, a real star, making a lot of trouble around town. You know I can make a five thousand dollar cash reward right now? Turn you in to the cops. Tell me why I shouldn't eh? Give me one good reason."

"I'm not the bad guy," I said. "Simple as that. I got set-up. I was running perimeter security for the star when she got ambushed up the street. Someone shot me off my bike right out in front of your restaurant that was conveniently closed for business that night. You know all this, we've been over this before. And now I'm absolutely certain that the sniper did the job from the top floor corner window of the building across the street. I was just there, I saw the evidence."

"So what? What does that matter? You got a photograph of the guy, you know what he looks like, was there a camera filming him when he was doing the shooting? Cause there sure is a lot of footage of you shooting people and places."

"When's the last time you got jumped and just stood there and took it?" I pointed at him. "That guy deserved worse than I gave him. Bottom line, I'd say he got off lucky."

"Bottom line, get the hell out of here. I don't need any more trouble." He pointed at the door.

"Just one question, and then I'll leave. Who owns the building across the street?"

He smiled, but it wasn't really a happy smile, more like a sly smile bordering on Oriental revenge. "Some big shot A-hole developer, name of Charles Washington."

I grimaced and caught my breath and nodded, that guy again.

He saw through my reaction.

"Why, you know him?"

"I guess I was working for him that night you found me. He was the one paying for the protection."

"Well you sure screwed that up."

"Sure did. But what do you have against

him? And why is that building so run down if they're trying to sell it?"

He scoffed. "They're not trying to sell it. They're trying to run us out of here."

I squinted my eyes and cocked my head. "What?"

"This whole block is owned by Charles Washington, both sides of the street, except for this building, we own it outright, no mortgage. You see my Grandpa out there sweeping the steps? He bought it over fifty years ago when he was a young man, worked his tail off to pay it off. We're free and clear, and we're not moving. The big shot developer thinks if he can keep the block run down, he can run us out of business, make it too dangerous for customers to come here for dinner. He wants to take over this whole block, bust it down completely and develop it into a high dollar destination, movie theatres and boutique restaurants and hotels, and nightclubs. We told him go ahead, we'll fit right in, we'll even help him, an authentic Chinese restaurant in the middle of his destination is a perfect scenario, but he is stubborn as a jackass, or a kid that won't share his candy bar. Wants it all or nothing, and so this street wallows in filth from his abandoned buildings."

"I remember a saying my old man used to have. He'd cut off his nose to spite his face."

The Chinese guy nodded. "Yeah, that he would. Now get out." He pointed to the door again. He never even said please, a hard case to the end.

I shrugged my shoulders. “Alright, I’m going. I got the answers I needed. You’re kind of like a fortune cookie that talks. Hard to crack open though.”

“I crack back,” he said and walked to the door and held it open for me.

I wouldn’t doubt it.

20.

It was an hour before midnight when I got to the center of the city. Skyscrapers rising from the asphalt and concrete all around me, and I found a parking space two blocks from the white gleaming tower of glass and steel nicknamed the Ivory Tower. Brand new, eighty floors of prime office and apartment space.

It was a perfect parking spot on the right hand of the street with a coin meter, twenty five cents per half hour, I could feed it coins all night if needed. I had a straight line of sight right into the front entrance of the building and most of the windows all the way to the top. At street level was a hotel type porte-cochere that could fit twenty full size busses, but they kept it clear of cars, I could see the doorman directing traffic in and out. I could lean the seat back and focus the scope on the entrance by looking under the steering wheel and if I wasn't careful I might fall asleep being too comfortable.

I had to admit it was a pretty busy front entrance, all types of people going in and out, mostly well-dressed business types, a lot of suits and ties and high heels. Taxis and limos pulled in and out and they had a valet parking attendant at a little stand on the side who would take cars to what must have been an parking facility under the building.

I figured that I would scope the entrance for a while, get a feel for it, the general vibe that was emanating from the center of it, and figure out a way to get in without being detected. The entrance to a building is like a talking mouth on a person, what you hear coming out of someone's mouth is what is coming directly from their soul in many ways, coming straight from their inside. If you see mean spirited people coming out of the entrance, then you have a mean spirited building.

I remembered back in Baghdad during the surge, there was this one little apartment building out towards the western part of the city. It had a good reputation, no one living there was a problem as far as we knew, but there were random mortar and firearms attacks nearby at odd days and times, hit and runs, and the intel we had pointed to the general area where this particular apartment building was located and so we set up a perimeter one night, an observation post to gather more intelligence, and I was scoping the entrance when I noticed that a significant percentage of the people going in and out of the building seemed angry, not yelling and spitting and cursing, but it was their eyes and their body language, the way the held their head and their limbs, their eyes looked angry, seething, they were tense all over, I could see it, I knew what it was, anger and turmoil boiling over inside of them and coming out through their eyes and posture.

Now of course we were in the middle of an occupied city in a war zone and most of the people in that city were either terrified or angry or both, so my theory was in it's infancy, but I made a note of it and talked to the Captain in charge of the platoon and he ordered a midnight raid, and sure enough we found a hidden stash of weapons in the cellar, maps of the city with marks on it where recent attacks had been made. These bad guys were keeping notes of where and when they ambushed coalition forces.

Tonight however, the people going in and coming out of this building seemed relaxed and happy, unstressed and cool. I rubbed my tired eyes and yawned. Maybe I was like a dog that was barking up the wrong tree. There was nothing here.

And then I brought the scope to bear on the entrance again and I saw this tall brooding guy with short hair walk slowly out the front doors, and it was the way he walked out, his entire body language and the way his eyes quickly scanned the edges of his vision, seemingly ready to jump out of the way of danger if it came at him out of nowhere, he was poised and balanced as if he could instantly spring in any direction if needed like a cat.

His face was serious, not seething and

angry, but all business. He slid over to the wall, out of the open and kept to the corners of the building as he moved. He looked like he was military grade, special forces, trained in weapons, survival, and hand to hand combat, and I recognized him from Baghdad. It was Parnell. First Lieutenant Justice Parnell, Fifth Army Division in one of the platoons in the Green Zone during the surge. He was a sniper and one of the best we had. He might have even saved my life one night.

It was a three platoon raid on an entire city block. A little after midnight we cordoned the whole place off and started knocking down doors, dragging guys out into the street. We were hustling to our portion of the block when a couple of guys on a motorcycle flew out of a nearby alley, scaring the hell out of us, and we scattered for cover, the guy on the back was ready to fire a rocket propelled grenade at us, he had it aimed and was pulling the trigger, when he seemed to be yanked right off the back of the bike, and the RPG went straight up into the air and came down in the middle of the street and exploded. He'd been shot off the motorcycle and the driver lost control and crashed into a telephone pole.

The motorcycle took us completely by surprise and none of us in the platoon had fired a shot, we all confirmed it on the spot as we re-grouped. Each platoon had a dedicated sniper on a nearby roof top with a straight line of sight to our target location and since we weren't at our target location yet, we surmised it must have been one of the other platoon's snipers.

"I'll bet Parnell got him," said my buddy, and we never really found out. It was on a need to know basis, and we weren't on the list of people needing to know anything. I tried to sit down next to him one day at lunch in the mess hall and introduced myself.

He was a real cool character, eyes set close together with a flat forehead, square jawed and it was the eyes, blackish brown and they had no sparkle of life in them, I remember they looked dull and he sort of gazed at me as I introduced myself.

"I'm Badger, fifth platoon, mind if I sit down sir?" He looked away and didn't say a word, just kept eating his beef stew and potatoes and watching the TV on the other side of the room, and so I cautiously set my tray down and sat across and one seat over from him so I wouldn't crowd him. "I think we owe you one sir. The other night when we raided the city block some guys on a motorcycle with an RPG came out of an alley, and a sniper took them out? Some of the guys said it might have been you."

He finished chewing, sucked in through one of his side teeth, and slowly looked back over at me.

"What'd you say your name was?"

"Badger sir, Badger Thompson, fifth platoon."

He nodded and then spoke very slowly and firmly, his eyes like pits filled with black stones. "Now listen here Badger Thompson fifth platoon, I don't talk about my kills, to anyone, ever. What's in the past is in the past. And that's where I want it all to stay. Understood?"

"Yes sir," I said. War didn't always bring out the best in people. Sometimes in a war zone you'll come across people that are dulled by the overwhelming experience, worn down mentally and physically by the horrible sights and sounds of people being killed and maimed on a daily basis, and they don't want to remember anything. They try with all their might to hide it all in some dark unused back corner of the labyrinth of their minds and block it out as best they can. All that effort, and the stress of constantly thinking that your number might come up next, and you get people that are borderline walking zombies, unable to carry on a normal conversation. Or it could be that they're just natural born jackasses and their true nature is on full display for all to see. I couldn't figure out which peg this guy fit. But I figured it was probably the latter when he turned his head back to the TV and said simply:

"Now you can leave."

Giving me permission to vacate the table.

Justice Parnell, sharpshooter, army sniper, coming out of the headquarters of the guy who owned the building where I was shot off my bike a couple of days ago. What a coincidence. I checked my weapons and got out of the car and stretched my legs for a stroll down memory lane. Time to re-acquaint myself with an old buddy.

He walked around the building and down

the street, and I followed. This was an upscale part of the city and prime real estate as it was, the street was lined with posh restaurants and shops, clothing boutiques and art galleries, most of which were still open, especially the bar and restaurant combos, winding up their dinner hours and heading into the early night cap hours with expensive cognacs and ports flowing into glasses while the money flowed the other way, into the cash register. Each of the establishments had a combo doorman security guy at the front, times being what they are these days and I pulled the cowboy hat low over my eyes while enduring suspicious stares from a couple of them.

Following someone is an art form in a way, whether it's in the middle of the uncharted wilderness or a well-travelled street the theory is the same, stay close enough to keep them or their trail in sight, but don't let them know that they're being stalked.

Parnell had a funny way of walking, he zigzagged down the sidewalk, walking slowly for a while and then speeding up, sometimes next to the buildings, and then out onto the curb, walking close to the cars parked on the sides, and every few zigs or zags he'd casually look back as though he'd dropped something, or was thinking of going back into an establishment that he'd just passed. He'd stop and lean against a lamppost and look down at his watch, and then start his zigzag walk again. Haphazardly making his way wherever it was he was going.

He was watching for a tail, and I kept far in the background, at least a block behind, sometimes more. My old cowboy hat was a giveaway, easily marked in the thin crowd that I was flowing with, and I took it off and left it on a car's windshield.

He walked slow and I walked slower, he turned to look at his watch or back down the street and I was already stopped and reading a billboard, squinting at the writing, or rummaging through a trash can like a bum, non-threatening and in my own dismal world as far as he could see, my eyes were never looking forward and I moved with peripheral vision. I shuffled as though I could barely walk, and needed new shoes and a bath. My head would tilt to the side from time to time like I was hearing voices or had a nervous tick. I was the crazy bum in the crowd, and would probably be picked up by the cops soon, or be asleep in an alley with an empty bottle of cheap wine in my lap. Non-threatening.

He stopped for an unusual amount of time, looking at his watch and back down the street and I blended into a small crowd of tourists, and from the corner of my eyes could see him slip into the front entrance of a posh apartment building. I made sure he wasn't peering around the edge of the entrance and I picked up my pace, still not looking straight ahead and moving with my peripherals but moving quickly now I closed the gap.

It was an open entrance that lead to a wide flight of stairs in the middle and a single elevator on the right hand side. The elevator indicator, green digital numbers showed that it was moving up, two three four, and it stopped on the fifth floor and stayed there. Maybe he was there to pick something up and would be taking the elevator back down, or maybe he would be staying put at one of the rooms on the fifth floor.

I made a quick choice and made for the stairway. Taking two steps at a time I was up three flights in less than half a minute and got blindsided as was I heading up to the fourth floor. He was crouched behind a wall next to the stairway and caught me with a kick to my knee that sent me sprawling into the railing and he was on me. My head hit the second stair while my chest imploded on the first stair knocking the wind out me and I saw stars shooting from the sides of my eyeballs while he got me in a headlock from behind.

"Why are you following me?" he whispered in my ear as he put the torque on my neck.

How in the hell did he expect me to answer while he had his forearm jammed into my windpipe was beyond me. I was running out of air, my lungs burning.

"I'm visiting a friend," I wheezed with my last full breath and he increased the pressure on my throat.

"Wrong," he hissed.

He was a top notch sniper but a lot of times those kind of guys neglect the hand to hand combat aspect of the equation. Sure they can end you from long distances, but get them up close and they have weaknesses, flaws in their armor. I wrapped my back right leg around his right leg that was splayed out for support and he tried to keep his balance as his foot was slipping on the ground, and then took off his front right hand that was pulling on his arm wedged across my throat and punched me once in the side of the head, and once in the mouth. Wrong move. He'd given up the locking part of his choke hold and I made him pay for it, circling my left arm up and around his left arm and flipping him over onto his back on the stairway.

"My turn," I said and continued flipping him till I had his back and almost had him locked in a full naked choke hold until he blocked me with an elbow and flipped *me* around, the bastard. He pulled a gun from a shoulder holster and tried to get a shot at me and I karate chopped down on his wrist and the gun fell out of his hand and clattered on the ground, but not before a shot rang out.

"Badger," he scowled and fell to the ground clutching his stomach.

"Parnell," I spit blood from my broken lip, and kicked the gun away. "Shot anyone off a motorcycle lately?"

"You're supposed to dead."

"Surprise."

"Kevlar vest?"

I nodded. "Double layer on the backside. Somehow I must have known a back stabber like you would try to get me from behind."

"That wouldn't have saved you from the car

bomb."

"How'd you know about that? So that was you too, huh?" I shook my head. "How'd you even know I had a car there? I parked it there once and never went back."

"We've been watching you for half a year." He grinned when he saw my reaction. "We watched you park it there, I knew what it was for, a weapons stash. What, did you think we planned this overnight? Hell, We know everything about you. When we found out you were still alive and then escaped from the hospital we rigged the car. I knew you'd head straight there, but I didn't have time to monitor the results."

"Too bad some punk kids tried to steal it before I got there."

"Yeah too bad about that."

"So you're the guy who kidnapped Gale? Does her billionaire boyfriend know about it?"

"You know how much they pay us grunts after serving our country. Putting our lives on the line. We come back and we're like beggars in the street. Highly trained beggars. Well I'm not gonna take scraps from the rich man's table Badger. If I see an opportunity I'm gonna get it."

"What the hell happened to you over there, in Iraq?"

He coughed from deep in his chest, and blood bubbled out of the corner of his mouth and out of his nostrils, and he laid his head back on the ground. "I died there."

His face was turning white and his hands

began to tremble.

"I better get you an ambulance," I said.

"Too late," he wheezed.

"Where's the girl?" I asked him. "Where's Gale Nighting?" I reached over and grabbed both his shoulders and gently shook him. "Where is she?"

"I don't know," he whispered and closed his eyes. "I did what I had to do. I did my job. Follow the money..."

And just like that he stopped breathing, a final slow breath whistled out of his mouth the sound getting smaller and smaller till it faded to nothing, and his hands became still and cold. I took the stairs down two at a time and slid out of the building with my cap over my eyes.

21.

Follow the money, Parnell said it with his last words. It was an old cliché and people bandied it around like a common phrase, but at one time it really hit home and meant something big. It was from the seventies, and the Watergate investigations, dirty tricks and political espionage, governments taken down by simply following the money being handed around to cover up crimes. Dirty money, hush money. Influential people with a lot of cash held sway over corrupt politicians and police and could get away with murder.

Alright, I'll follow the money.

At the present time the most money in the immediate vicinity was sitting at the top of the ivory tower in the back pocket of one Charles H. Washington the second. I wondered what kind of man Charles the first was, humble and kind, or ostentatious and flamboyant like the second. Maybe something in between. And how in the hell did he get a name with 'the second' on it when everyone knew he was an orphan? Was he really a second, or did he just add that title to his name so he could be cool with all his rich friends, to fit in at the country club.

What traits carried over in the gene pool from his real Dad, the bum, to the guy sitting on all that cash at the top of the tower?

I thought my own Dad then, raising me up as best as he could on his own, with a steady stream of part time temporary Moms on the side. Some good, some worse than a proverbial snake in the grass, like the one who we caught stealing my lunch money of all things.

He had an old saying whenever he was going to teach me or show me something new that he thought I'd need in the future. It usually went something like this: "Say pal, have you ever jumped off a cliff? No? Well this is your lucky day!" He'd pound his fist into his open hand, crack his knuckles and laugh as he said it.

Whenever he told me this was going to be my lucky day, it usually meant I was going to get my ass kicked. He told me straight up many times: you make your own luck, it was *never* just handed to you.

One day we took a ride down to the beach and the waves were giant and scary, rising up and crashing on the sand. I was young, maybe five years old when he pulled it on me the first time, but I remembered that day like it was yesterday. He pulled into the parking lot in front of Laguna Beach and pointed to the ocean.

“Say pal,” he asked. “Have you ever played chicken with the waves?” I shook my head no.

“You haven’t? Well this is your lucky day.” And I got excited since lucky days sounded like good days. And then his voice got low and conspiratorial, like we were in on a secret together.

“You see, you wait until there’s a lull and no waves at all, the water receding back, and you get as close to the ocean as you can and when a big wave comes along you wait as long as you can stand it, the longer you wait, the braver you are, and then run like hell and hope it doesn’t catch up to you.”

It sounded like a lot of fun, and we went down to the edge of the ocean and it was just like he said, the water receded and we went as close as we could, but when the giant wave came at us towering above me, my little legs couldn’t run fast enough up the beach and it picked me up and ground me head first into the sand with a ton of water grabbing at me and swirling around and just about drowning me, then dragged me back down the steep beach into the maelstrom for another drubbing that went on and on for an eternity.

My good old Dad finally dragged me by the seat of my pants out of the soup and up the beach and we both caught our breath in great gulps.

“I thought we was goners,” he said, and scratched his head like he’d just learned a life lesson. “I guess that’s why they say never turn your back on a wave.” Then he winked at me with a twinkle in his eye. "Want to go again?"

All these things I pondered in the back of my mind as I studied the building and the entrances, and windows, and guards stuffed here and there, some visible, some invisible. This was a fortress.

I felt like my Dad was looking down at me from Heaven and telling me that this was my lucky day. I could almost hear him pounding his fist into his hand and cracking his knuckles.

With my night scope I could clearly see the doorman at the entrance, opening doors when cars entered the Porte-cochere, directing traffic, he was packing a big gun, I could see the bulge at his waist under the coat.

Just inside the quadruple sized glass slider doors sat a security guard with a white shirt and tie, gold private security badge, sitting on a big stool, tapping his foot, and wearing a gun on his hip right out in the open for everyone to see. Parked to the side in a black sedan with tinted windows and the driver's side window down sat a guy in a black suit and tie and shades.

He looked menacing enough with a pock marked face and square jaw, but it was hard to tell if he was watching the entrance or was asleep. These are the guys that I could see, and as I scanned the surrounding area I saw little places and cubby holes that could have more security stashed and ready. The invisible ones, the perimeter.

I knew that if I had this guy's money, and the way the world really was, I'd have a sniper team positioned on the second floor in both of the buildings that looked over the front and rear entrances with infra-red scopes, and long range metal detectors, while inside the building itself I'd have explosive device sniffers hidden in the walls, full-body-scan cameras in the doorframes hooked up to x-ray machines in a side room. A couple of German Shepherds in dog houses by the front and back entrances ready to attack on command. Train them night and day to smell a thief or a terrorist. No one would get near this building with a gun or a bomb unless it was *my* idea to bring one in.

Reality came into focus, and I realized without a doubt that there was no way I was going to penetrate the security of this place on my own, not tonight anyways, and I threw that idea out the proverbial door. If I was going to penetrate this building, I needed a team that could hit five points at once, create lot of misdirection and then, and maybe only then I'd have a chance to slip in un-noticed.

I'd have to be patient and wait it out.

If I wanted to talk to this guy I'd have to bunker down and wait till he left his fortress, and follow him and catch him without the bulk of his security contingent hovering around him. Catch him with his pants down so to speak.

Catch him and do what?

Ask him what he did with his girlfriend to start with. Might as well. As deep as I was into this I might as well go right to the top and see if this guy had something to do with it. After all, wasn't that what the police normally did with missing person cases? Look at those people who were closest to the missing first and foremost? The friends, the family, the husband or the boyfriend. Only in this case they had a convenient fall guy, a big dummy, a patsy who everyone thought must be the guilty one.

Me.

I waited and watched. It was half past midnight now, the time of night my old Dad warned me about, the bottom half of the night, and the type of people that were out and about had a different vibe around them. The bottom feeders.

I saw robbers and winos and party animals. Hookers and pimps, and drug dealers and users, along with some basic hardworking honest people who were on their way home, or to a midnight job to pay the bills.

People that were heading to a graveyard shift, or heading to the graveyard.

Traffic was thinner but it had more of an edge to it. Something was about to go down. The hair on the back of my neck was standing on end and I focused the night scope on the scene in front of me.

There was movement at the porte-cochere. The uniformed security guard got out of his chair and stood at attention by the door while the doorman waved to the white limo and it pulled up to the glass doors, and then out of the building walked a thin dark well-dressed man in a sport suit and tie. He nodded to the uniformed security guard and stood talking to the doorman for a moment and then got into the back seat of the limo. The dark sedan pulled in behind the limo and both cars drove out of the porte-cochere and onto the highway, heading my way. They were on the move and so was I.

As they passed by I turned my head to the side to shield my face, then started the car and made my way onto the highway and did a U-turn, heading northwest on Wilshire. I kept ten car lengths behind them and a couple of cars in between, and then a slow poke in a lime green electric car pulled in front of me and slowed down to the speed limit of all things, and the limo was getting way too far in front so I pulled into the right lane and passed the slow poke.

Not a good maneuver if you're following someone, it was a red flag for the security detail if they were watching for a tail, but there was nothing I could do. I had to stay close. The slow poke flipped me off as I passed him, some old hippie in a tie dye shirt and bandana, and I checked my urge to show him a gun barrel.

Ten minutes of driving and we were on the outskirts of La Brea. My newest favorite town. Beautiful downtown La Brea, tar pits and rap clubs and jealous boyfriends with guns. The limo and sedan turned down a side street and I followed as far behind as I could. This was familiar territory, unfortunately.

In neon lights in the distance the sign on the side of the building said simply, 'The Pit'. The rap club that I was most likely banned from for life.

They probably had my picture on the wall by the front door with a bullseye on my face and the caption: 'Shoot on Sight'.

I parked on the corner two blocks from the club and pulled out my night scope. The limo parked directly in front of the front entrance under the neon lights, with the black sedan nestled neatly behind it's bumper. Charles Washington got out of the limo and it looked like he was talking to the doorman, who looked very serious and nodded his head at whatever was being said to him. It was a different doorman than the one that took a shot at me last night and got a couple in his ankles in return. This guy looked bigger, calmer, and tougher.

I was in no hurry, in fact the longer C-Dub stayed up the better my odds were of catching him and his security team dozing. Stay up till dawn for all I care you bastard, I'll catch you right before the sun rises when you're at your most vulnerable.

Maybe he was going in for a nightcap or two, which would be even better. Invite your crew in and give them a couple of drinks while you're at it. But he didn't go into the club, instead walking alone across the street to the boarded up and darkened tattoo parlor. It was a two story box shaped building, large display windows on the bottom floor and small windows on the second floor.

The limo driver and the two guys from the sedan stood next to the cars laughing and joking about something with the doorman. The doorman however wasn't laughing and the joke was obviously at his expense. I swung the scope over to the tattoo parlor as C-Dub opened the front door and then closed it behind him. I switched to infrared and could see him through the side windows climbing stairs inside the dark building and then on the second floor a dim light went on in one of the interior rooms.

His two-man security team started walking towards the front door of the club, and went inside leaving their boss unprotected.

The light in the second floor window of the tattoo parlor was still on, and even though there were curtains across the window, I could see shadows moving across the wall inside the room. Time for me to go, and I took a deep breath, checked my weapons and got slowly out of the car. My plan was simple, go around the block and come in on the alleyway next to the tattoo parlor and find a way in.

I strolled nonchalantly across the street being careful not to limp, and then hustled around the block and found myself at the alleyway next to the parlor. It was dark and narrow with trash cans and cars and it smelled like oil and piss and wet garbage.

I startled a bum who was trying to sleep between two parked cars with a bunched up newspaper for a pillow. He mumbled something unintelligible and laid his head back down in the gutter.

I was nestled in the darkness of the alleyway, pressing my body against the brick wall as I walked halfway down the alley now, heading for window and door near the front of the building. Lined up perfectly like I was a bullet inside the barrel of a gun aimed at the other side of the street and the entrance to the club, the limo and the sedans and the doorman standing alone. He seemed to look over to the alley now and then but there's no way he could see me with my dark clothes and black beanie over my head and half my face.

The window was a foot from the wooden door which was thick and old and locked. The bottom of the window was at shoulder height, three feet square and boarded with two by fours that were fastened with deck screws just like the ones that I saw at the building by the Chinese restaurant. I wondered why they didn't use ply board like that other building. Maybe they ran out. The boards, three in all went straight up and down like the bars on a prison cell. I'd have to pry at least two off to get at through the window but I forgot to bring my crowbar and I made a mental note to include that item the next time I wanted to break into an abandoned building.

I didn't have a crowbar, but I had a knife, a very sharp knife and I pulled it from the side of my boot. The handle was thick and grippy and fit perfectly into the palm of my hand. With enough time, I could cut down an oak tree, but I didn't have much time and this was no oak tree.

The window frame was made of two by four wood and I started carving it right next to where the wooden prison bars were attached. Carving and slicing on the window frame until the wood came off like a slice of turkey on Thanksgiving day with the deck screws still attached. I carved the bottom portion of two of the wooden prison bars free from the building and then pried them up and away so I could crawl under them.

Now I could get in through the window, but I still had the window itself to contend with. Two glass panes where one slid up and over the other and was latched in the middle. It too was locked. It was the kind of lock that was as big as your thumb and shaped like a half moon that you pulled with a knob and rotated open. I wedged the knife blade between the panels and with the point of the blade sticking straight into the metal sliding bolt started working it open a millimeter at a time and within a few seconds I was in. The window opened a crack with the release of tension on the lock and I opened it enough so I could crawl up and in.

There was a metal table under the window and I cautiously put some weight on it while keeping my shoulders and arms on the inside of the window sill until I was clear and had my feet secure on the ground. The bottom floor was still and dark and I could hear my heart beating in the silence.

Somewhere above on the second floor was the faint sound of people talking. Dimly resonating through the walls and down the stairway. Two distinct voices, with diverging cadences and tones, both masculine and I'd hoped to hear the sound of a girls voice, or none at all. Someone was with C-Dub, maybe one of his security guys had come through the front while I was sneaking in the side, and if I wanted to get some answers out of him I'd have to deal with the other guy first most likely.

The sound of a door opened and heavy footsteps on the landing and then coming down the stairs towards the front of the store. I slid quickly to the bottom and side of the stairs and crouched, waiting. My eyes were used to the darkness, but the other guy coming out of a lit room and down darkened stairs was at a disadvantage, he didn't see me till it was too late.

Karate chop, L-18 neck ligament swift and clean, and I held him up with one hand over his mouth and my arm around his neck and lowered him gently to the ground, his knees folding under him like a marionette with his strings cut from above.

It wasn't one of the guys from the security detail in the sedan that followed the limo to the club. This guy was thinner and wiry, with a short haircut, a military cut. Just like Parnell. Maybe this was another one of the hit squad. I searched his pockets and found a small pistol with a silencer attached to the barrel that went straight into my back pocket. I pulled him back into the shadows and pressed my thumbs into the knock out points to give me a few extra minutes.

I could hear some movement in the room at the top of the stairs, a piece of furniture being moved, and then a voice began talking low and slow, one voice, one cadence, one inflection. Maybe he was talking to himself I thought, or on the phone to someone, it sounded like he was giving instructions, and I slid over to the front of the stairway and started walking up, wary of a loose step and a squeak that would give me away. I stayed away from the center of the stairs and made my way up the left side. I stepped carefully and quietly, putting all my weight on the leading foot only when I was sure that no sound would come from the action.

The door at the top of the stairs was open just a crack, enough to let out a sliver of golden light and I kept to the side of the stairway as I climbed, and crouched ever so slightly and blending into the handrail in case someone on the other side of the street could see through the boarded up windows and sound the alarm. I was at the top now and hovered near the wall and creeping nearer to the door so I could finally see inside. The voice was clearer now, methodical and cruel.

"You didn't think I'd find out what you did? You think I'm stupid? All this time building my empire, my reputation and you thought you could tear me down? Take me for a ride? Nobody messes with me and gets away with it, nobody. When I get finished with you they won't find a single piece of flesh from your body, they'll only find bones, brittle and whitened and broken, bits and pieces here and there and everywhere, like a jigsaw puzzle.

When I get *halfway* finished with you, you'll wish you were never born, you'll yell it out loud with a muffled scream and no one will hear you."

A piece of furniture was being moved again, as though he was rising from a chair and pushing it away. It seemed as though he was talking on the phone to someone, threatening them. If I could catch him with his back to the door and mid-sentence I could immobilize him and get some answers out of him. I peered through the crack in the door. He was standing next to an empty chair, probably the one he'd been sitting in, standing there and looking down at another chair that was not empty. He continued on.

"You didn't think I'd find out about your little boyfriend down in Rio? Your little cabana boy you picked up by the pool last month on tour. The penniless towel boy. Didn't think I would find out did you? Making a fool out of me." He spit on the floor in front of her.

The girl in the chair, bound and gagged with long brown hair and terrified blood shot and tear filled eyes shook her head and pleaded with a mute voice. It was the star. The Nightingale. He had a gun in his hand, it looked like a Glock with a silencer and he put the barrel next to her cheek and shook his head.

"Tsk tsk tsk. You should have known better Gale. But that's okay, it's all going to work out for the best for everyone, except for you that is, and cabana boy, we'll take care of him later, I'll send someone down to pay him a visit when this is over and done with. It's actually very, very good that I found out who you really are, a backstabbing money grubbing wench like the rest of them. It's good that I found out, it really is. You see I traded you in for something much better, traded up in fact, I traded you, your records, your voice, your life's work which I own like I own a slave, traded you in for a piece of one of the biggest sports franchises in the world. The timing actually couldn't have been much better. If I hadn't found out about your little betrayal, there's no way I would have parted with you. No way. But now? Well let's just say it's all over except for the crying. My deal is done, I sold the record company earlier this evening, inked the contract, got the money transferred into my account and now all I need to do is negate my contract with you. Sever my ties so to speak. Financially, it doesn't matter to me now whether you live or die. But in here," he tapped on his chest. "Spiritually, it does matter. We're taking you out of here in a box, taking you somewhere far out in the desert where the coyotes roam and if someone ever does find you, they won't even know what they're looking at."

Unfortunately for me, I thought, if she was never found, I would be a fugitive for life, or worse.

Also unfortunate right now was the fact that she was facing the door that I needed to open and confront this piece of crap madman.

If I opened it slowly so I could get a jump on him, her eyes would betray me and he might have the advantage. He also might kill her suddenly and they could still pin the blame on me somehow.

I needed her safe and sound and very much alive. If I came out with my gun blazing, she might get hit, he might get a shot off, you never knew. I was going to have to grapple him.

C-Dub paced the floor with his pistol pointed down, thinking, scratching his chin and pondering, scratching and pondering some more. He seemed ready to lecture her again about what she did and what he was going to do.

He walked in front of her blocking my view of her, and her of me and I swung the door open and lunged at him, both my hands free and I grabbed his wrist and pinned his gun arm at his side and twisted it like a crank and pulled it behind his back, gun still pointing down, his trigger finger should have been immobile but he was able to get a shot off and the sound of the bullet hitting the wood floor with a crack was much louder than the muffled sound from the silencer.

I snapped his wrist down and the gun clattered away, then with my hip on his back and my hand around his neck I tried to Judo flip him onto the floor, but my left leg was too weak from last night's gunshot and he was too quick, and I could tell right away that he was trained in martial arts as he slipped out of my upper throat grip with a backside flipper move and rotated low and took my feet out from under me with a leg sweep.

I fell on my back cursing with my gun squirting out from the holster and he was on top of me straddling me and trying to land blows with his fists, and I reached up and brought him closer to minimize the damage and grappled, pulling on his shoulders to minimize the distance.

I closed the space between his fists and my face and he had no room to wind up and the blows were ineffective and weak, I reached up with my thumbs in his eye sockets ready to blind him but he blocked my hands down and I was able to bring my good leg up and around his face and leverage him off me while nearly breaking his neck.

He sprang off me like a cat crouching and ready to attack and I stayed low ready to repel him, both our guns were lying on the ground behind me by the window, and I tried to shuffle backwards and reach for one of them.

He rushed at me full speed with a strange growling sound coming from his throat, then Gale reached out an untethered foot as he passed by her, tripping him and he stumbled towards me wildly trying to regain his balance, bringing his right fist high in the air with the intent to bring it straight down on my head and I ducked low under the blow and used his inertia against him, harnessed his forward momentum and redirected his trajectory and body blocked him up and through the window.

The glass shattered and he flew through

the black night air into the alley below, so startled that he couldn't even grab enough air into his lungs to scream and he hit with a dull sickening thud on the street below, shards of glass raining down on him with a tinkling sound.

I looked down and through the broken window at the crumpled body below, arms and legs at broken angles and a dark pool of blood spreading from his head that was face down on the black asphalt. I was breathing hard from the fight and I exhaled and tried to calm myself, it wasn't over yet.

I pulled the gag off and untied the knots that held Gale to the back of the chair, she was sobbing and trembling in fear, tears streaming down her face and she threw her arms around me and I held her for a moment and stroked the back of her head.

"There there, it's okay now, he's gone from this world. Can you stand up? Can you walk?" I looked into her eyes. "My name is Badger, I was on the security detail when you got kidnapped. I was on the perimeter but a sniper took me out before I could help. I'm here to get you out of here." I could see by her eyes that she trusted me. I asked her again. "Can you walk?"

"I think so." Her voice was soft and halting.

I pulled the phone out from my back pocket, it was broken in two, and a quick scan of the room convinced me it was a risky waste of time to look for another one. It would have been nice to call for some back-up, the police, fire department, anyone.

"Now listen," I told her. "There are some very bad men downstairs, and we have to get away from them and get you to the police. Let's see if you can stand up and walk."

I pulled her to her feet and she was weak and nearly fainted so I gently sat her right back down.

She was a small woman, and I estimated that she might weigh around ninety five or a hundred pounds on a good day which this wasn't and they'd probably starved her for a couple of days by the looks of her hollowed out cheeks. I could carry her to the car.

I hustled over to the window and picked up the two pistols and tucked one into my holster and the other into my back pocket and went over and lifted her up into my arms. "I'll carry you like a sack of potatoes," I joked and she tried to smile through the tears. "Put your arms around my neck and hold on tight."

Broken ribs and shot leg be damned, I picked her up and carried her across the wooden floor, closed the door behind us and went down the dark stairs one at a time feeling with my toes in my shoes before committing to the next step, slowly making our way down. When we got about halfway down the stairs I could see through some cracks in the boarded up windows at the front of the store, and the club across the street.

The two security guys had come back out and were talking with the club's bouncer again.

One of them was looking this way. He'd take a puff on a cigarette, look this way then look away again. He motioned with his cigarette to the others and I could imagine him asking them what was taking so long and maybe they should go check on their boss.

We got to the bottom floor and went to the right towards the alleyway and the side entrance. There was a scuffling sound as the guy I'd knocked out earlier was trying to get up, regaining consciousness. I didn't have time to give him another dose of L-18 therapy and soccer kicked him once in the side of his chin and he slumped on the floor and was silent again.

"That's the guy you were asking about," I whispered to her. "He won't be following us."

The side door was locked with a dead bolt on the side and a button in the middle of the handle and I was able to reach down and unlock both and wrestle open the door. It must have been shut for a long time, it was stuck on the frame and popped open with some extra effort, the hinges squeaking lightly, and I hissed through my teeth at the sound.

Out in the alley it was pitch black, the sound of the rap club resonated on the walls around us, and I kept close to the bricks and glanced back to see the security guy with cigarette take a last puff, throw the butt on the ground, grind it under his heel and start across the street towards the front entrance of the tattoo shop.

I picked up my pace. I figured I had about

two minutes before they figured out what had happened and started after us. We passed by C-Dub face down on the street and she turned her head and hid it in the nook of my shoulder. We turned the corner of the block and headed south, behind us in the alley there was a shout from the second floor window. My two minute estimate was way off. I hefted her up and threw her over my shoulder and half stumbled half ran to the southern corner of the block and headed for the car.

I set her into the passenger side, and whipped her seatbelt on and clicked it secure. There were more shouts from the corner of the block and at the front of the club.

The bouncer was yelling and pointing at us while one security guy ran down the street with his gun in the air and the other came around the corner of the building behind us and ran towards us while firing a large pistol. Not the best tactic for a good shot. Bullets ricocheted off the building behind us.

I pulled out my Glock, took careful aim and dropped him with one shot in the center of his neck.

Then I turned my attention to the other guy running at us from the club who must have realized what had happened to his partner around the corner, and ducked between two parked cars.

I fired one shot into the window of the car behind him to keep him down and it shattered onto the street, then I jumped into my little car, pushed Gale low into the seat, revved the engine once, and burned rubber out of there, tires squealing, smoke spewing, fighting the steering wheel, U-turning it to the south and away from the club.

The back window blew apart and a bullet whistled and ricocheted inside the car, skipping around inside before plugging into the dashboard above the radio, and I zigzagged down the street, gas pedal to the floorboard and then the engine popped and started misfiring and pinging, sounding like I was running short a piston, took a left turn down a side street heading east, the next street was Wilshire, the miracle mile and I was hoping for a miracle to get us to the police station.

Black smoke starting coming out of the exhaust pipe, I could see a cloud in the rear view mirror billowing behind us, and then it started seeping into the car from the engine compartment. Maybe the shooter hit the engine block with a lucky shot, or maybe I bought a lemon off the car lot. Either way this car was dying fast. I opened the windows to get the smoke out and behind us came the sound of screeching tires and honking horns, cars swerving out of the way of a white stretch limo gaining fast on us.

Another bullet shattered my side mirror. Up ahead was a row of stores, then a small strip mall, and a two story brick building that looked like a library, neat and trim and square with a flagpole out front and the sign at the front in bright blue letters said 'Police'.

The limo slammed into the back of my car

and I struggled to keep from spinning out of control, and turned the wheel to the right, tires screeching full-speed up the sidewalk and slammed on the brakes, turning the car sideways and crashing into the glass front door of the Police station.

The engine ground to a halt, sputtered and died with a cough, and there was a strange moment of complete silence. I turned my head to my left through the driver's side window, and saw the limo slow down, the driver and passenger looked at me grimly and then drove slowly down the road, pulled into traffic and sped away into the night. I reached out to pat Gale's shoulder and she looked at me with wide terrified eyes and while trembling said simply.

"I'm okay."

Then piles of blue uniformed cops came out of every nook and cranny with guns drawn while circling our smashed car. It was like I'd stirred up a colony of giant blue ants, and they were very, very angry.

I however, was happy and fairly smiling as I sighed deeply and put my hands flat with palms down on top of the dashboard and waited for them to pull me out of the smashed car, and cuff me and Taser me, and put their boots on my neck if they wanted to. We were safe.

Someday soon though I'd have to track down the two guys in the limo, before they tracked me down.

But for now, it was over.

EPILOGUE

You know how it is in the first hour of morning down by the docks. The fog hovers on the water, hanging close and still like a soft baby's blanket while the sun rises over the mountains, golden red and shining through the high cloud cover to the east. Not a whisper of wind. Sounds, which are few and far between, are magnified and important, setting themselves aside in your senses to be revered and listened to carefully.

The distant putt-putt of a motorboat leaving the safety of the harbor, the slap of water from its wake on the pilings, the boats lined up neatly in rows, all shapes and sizes, big and little, square and slender, fat and thin, powerboats and sailboats, work boats and play boats all gently squeaking against their rope tethers, metal lines tapping against a towering mast, a crow with it's strange cry on the brown grass hillsides behind while the seagulls circle call out to each other high in the sky above as they head out to sea.

The sharp smell of fish and salt and kelp, and a wisp of diesel from one of the work boats.

If you look carefully into the calm greenish blue water you can see small fish hiding by the barnacle covered pilings, both colorful and grey, some darting here and there, while others hover in an ethereal liquid dream. Everything seems at once magnificent and new at dawn at the harbor.

"What are you thinking about?" Amber poked me in my ribs and put her arm around my waist.

My gaze was to the East and the sunrise. I'd been thinking about the past couple of months, the unraveling of C-Dubs empire, the investigations and uncovering of the massive fraud, killings, cover-ups and broken lives and careers.

Mostly I was thinking about the two guys in the limo who'd gotten away, and whether they were going to show up someday, unannounced. But I didn't tell her any of those thoughts.

"I was thinking what a great day it's going to be on the water, out in the channel between here and Catalina." I smiled and poked her back. "And I was wondering which one we should take out."

I waved my hand like the host at beauty pageant towards the two gleaming white hulled boats that we were standing next to, their bows facing us, black letters on their backsides proudly proclaiming their names.

'Sugar' on the forty foot sleek double masted ketch with the sixty foot high center mast, and 'Spice' on the fifty foot power boat with the twin five hundred horsepower diesel engines, its fly bridge and tuna tower rising nearly to the height of the sailboat's mast.

"Hmmm." She tapped her finger on her chin and perused the question. "That's a tough one, and a nice problem to have."

In a twist of fate, Gale's business manager made sure that she had an insurance policy for kidnapping and ransom for her trip to South America where she met cabana boy and started this whole chain of trouble.

In the event she was kidnapped and there was a ransom demand, the insurance policy paid for it.

It would also be paid in the event that someone rescued her. Imagine that.

The half million dollar reward for the safe return of Nightingale was eventually awarded to me and was spent rather wisely I thought on the two vessels.

After taxes, the remaining quarter of a million dollars plus what I had saved was enough to purchase both of the boats at auction with enough left over to retro-fit them to almost new condition.

"I'm fine with either one," I said. "But I'm sort of feeling partial to filling the mainsail of the Sugar with some steady wind from the south while powering through the chop with a deep and heavy bowline."

She pointed at the red sunrise. "But what about the old saying, 'red sky in the morning, sailor's warning'?"

"Old wives tale." I countered. "Meant to

scare lily livered landlubbers into staying on shore and working in the fields. Now if the sky was red in the morning while the wind was blowing forty knots I'd say it was a warning well warranted and true. But not today young Amber, not today. I'll estimate the wind will get up to around..." I licked my index finger and put it high in the air while squinting hard at the sky. "...ten to fifteen knots in the middle of the channel." I winked at her. "Plus I read the weather report this morning."

"Cheater." She punched me in the arm.

"It's a nice day for a sail, maybe we should take Sugar, and we'll be at Catalina by mid-afternoon."

She smiled at that thought. "I'd love to go for a sail."

In the corner of my eye I saw a long white limo crawling ever so slowly along the wide boulevard fronting the entrance to the harbor, going too slow, too careful, the driver searching the hundreds of slips as he went along and turned in and headed down the road that bordered the wharf.

Was this the day? Were the two fugitives going to show up and exact their revenge on me? I always envisioned that it'd be somewhere in the middle of the night with them jumping out of the bushes at me. I was always ready, and the gun in the holster at my side was always loaded with the safety off.

"There they are!" she said excitedly and waved with her free hand to the driver of the limo who finally saw her and headed our way.

"I'm so proud of you." She gushed and reached up to kiss me on the cheek. "Your first customer."

And it was true, I had my very own protection service just like I'd dreamed. Today was the first official day of business.

The limo pulled up in front of us and I couldn't help but smile. Out stepped Gale Nighting and three of her best friends, two were guys and one was a girl. We were heading to Catalina for a party where she was the guest of honor and I was her bodyguard for the boat ride over and for the event. Gale shrieked and ran towards us and threw her arms around me, nearly choking me. Then she hugged Amber and turned to her friends and waved them over.

"I'd like you meet Rhonda, her boyfriend Garrett, and this is my new best friend..." her cheeks blushed as she pulled him closer to shake my hand. "This is Cody Markender."

He was some sort of mix and I couldn't put my finger on it, Jamaican, German and Filipino came to mind and I made a note to ask him when we were under way.

"Glad to meet you sir," he said and shook my hand. He had a firm grip, and I gave it back in kind.

He called me sir, either out of respect, or maybe I was looking rather old and rumpled and ragged around the edges this morning. He was a young sort after all, smooth skin, and clear eyes, maybe even too young to shave, and he had a little bounce to his stance, I noticed that he kept his knees bent a little, ready for fight or flight. Maybe he was trained in martial arts I thought, or just worried being this close to me. Something about him triggered a memory.

"You look familiar," I said. "Where have I seen you before?"

"Cody's in the recording industry," said Gale. "We met at the studio in New York where I'm making my new album, which by the way has a song I wrote about you." She was beaming.

"About me?" My eyes narrowed, suspicious.

"Don't worry," she laughed. "I'm not using your name or anything like that, just some of your actions." She made her hand stiff and karate chopped the air. "Your love knocks me out. Although we don't know if it will make it past the PC police. It might be too violent."

I smiled. "So I made it to the big leagues? That's an honor, thank you." I turned back to her new best friend and asked him. "So what type of music to you play?"

"Cody's a rap star!" Gale nearly shouted, and when my smile slowly turned to a frown, everyone laughed except for Cody when he saw my eyes.

Rap stars were trouble, and I squashed trouble with my bare hands if needed. I swore to myself after the C-Dub fiasco that if I ever saw another rap star I'd either head the other way or break their neck before they could start any trouble and smack talking.

The most worthless piece of garbage non-music waste of time and talent this world has ever seen.

Rap star. My mind went blank with anger and I clenched my fists.

He saw the look in my eyes and kept his knees bent for fight or flight and was quick with an explanation.

"I'm uh, going to branch out into different types of music, it's just a launching pad, sort of....sir" He swallowed with a dry gulping sound while beads of sweat popped out on his forehead.

I could see then and there, and without a doubt that he was a good kid, and that Gale was in good hands with him at her side. You can tell a lot of things about people with a first impression and their reaction to sudden adversity. Like having a pissed off guy like me near enough to put a karate chop on your neck.

It was at that very moment in time that I made a decision to help him see the world from my perspective, my point of view. To help him deal with the kind of mis-fortune and calamity that not many people have the opportunity to face. And to face it from a position of strength and confidence, not weakness and fear. I would train him, starting today. Some things had to be learned by doing.

"Can you swim?" I asked him.

He shrugged. "Sure, I can swim. Why?"

I put my hand on his shoulder and pointed to the sailboat sitting quietly at the edge of the dock.

"Have you ever trimmed a foresail in a

twenty knot wind, your feet slipping on the heaving deck of a ship hard at sea, while white water the size of haystacks are breaking over the bow and trying to knock you off the boat, ten long miles from the nearest dry land?"

He looked at me with a half-smile and a 'what are you kidding me' attitude, but the look in my eyes told him different.

The half-smile faded away as he realized he was trapped, and he tried to catch his breath while he looked from me to the sailboat, then back to me again, and he shook his head nervously, thinking carefully before replying.

"No."

I smiled at his answer, and walked towards the boat.

"Well, today's your lucky day."

The End.

Made in the USA
San Bernardino, CA
17 December 2016